If These WALLS Could TALK:
PITTSBURGH PENGUINS

Stories from the Pittsburgh Penguins Ice, Locker Room, and Press Box

Phil Bourque with Josh Yohe

30 YEARS
TRIUMPH
B O O K S

Library of Congress Cataloging-in-Publication Data available upon request.

This book is available in quantity at special discounts for your group or organization. For further information, contact:

Triumph Books LLC
814 North Franklin Street
Chicago, Illinois 60610
(312) 337–0747
www.triumphbooks.com

Printed in U.S.A.

ISBN: 978-1-62937-410-9

Design by Nord Compo

CONTENTS

FOREWORD

My whole family lives in California, so over the years, I can honestly say Phil Bourque has become a part of my family. He is my brother.

He and I are blessed to do something we love for a living, which is being around the great game of hockey. It's not a job to either one of us. It really isn't. It's simply a way of life, and I can tell you that being along for this ride with him for so many years has been one of the thrills of my lifetime. It's been exhilarating, something different every day. Every game is different. Every *day* is different. That's the beauty of the game, and I couldn't imagine having a better broadcast partner or friend to join me on this journey over the years. What an experience it's been to have him beside me in the broadcast booth for the better part of two decades.

To fully appreciate the job Phil does as a broadcaster is to fully appreciate the work he puts in. I don't know that there are any broadcasters in all of sports who are as dedicated and hardworking as this man. It's remarkable to see how prepared he is on a daily basis. I used to be so proud of myself because I'd have all these nuggets written down, things that you'd rarely hear me mention on the air, because I wanted to be more prepared than anyone. Now, he scares me, because he's got even more nuggets than I do! He's trumping me now. And he knows that I know. He never brags about it, but he knows I know, and I hope he also knows how proud I am of him.

I told him in the beginning that if he truly wanted to excel in this line of work, his knowledge from playing the game for so long and his natural charisma weren't enough. He needed to outwork everyone, just like when he was playing the game. At this point, I truly believe he is at the very top of his game as a broadcaster in the National Hockey League.

It's a tedious job at times, and yet I never hear him complain. He puts his head down and goes to work, and he's truly unmatched in my mind. He excels in every facet of the business. He's insightful,

Whether it's in the booth or on the road, always happy to have Mike Lange by my side. (Getty Images)

entertaining, prepared, and he's developed the ability to interview people well, which is no small task. I'm a sucker for good journalism more than I am charisma, and I can tell you that be brings both to the table. His growth has been something to behold, and it's going to be quite evident for the readers of this book. Phil is one of those people who gets better at anything when he puts his mind to it—except for golf, of course.

The players are a little different nowadays than they were when Phil played. They were a little wilder back then, but that was partly because they could be. There weren't smartphone cameras back then. Heck, there weren't even cellphones. Phil tells plenty of stories in this book, and I promise you they're all true. If Bourquey and I had been at the mercy of the smartphone generation of today, we both would have been in trouble.

We are together every day during the season and, during those long summers, I don't speak with him every day. But we do stay in touch even during those times, because that's just the kind of bond we have. We work together so well, and we've become so very close over the years. He's just a special guy, the kind of guy you want to be around all the time. He makes bad days a little better. He makes good days great. If you knew him, you'd like him.

When I think of Phil, I think of the word *passion*. He has the kind of passion that is rare. He has a true passion for his children more than anything else. He has a passion for the game of hockey. He has a passion for the Pittsburgh Penguins. He has a passion for broadcasting. And really, he has a passion for life. That's Phil Bourque.

He's the man of all answers, and you'll find that in this book. Need a travel tip? No one travels like the Ol' Two-Niner, so just ask him. He's Mr. Travel. Need the best rental car place? Ask him. The guy could be his own travel agency. He has lived the life, and what a story he has to tell. The stories alone are a reason to read this book. Who am I to challenge the array of hair-raising adventures that he has experienced? I could tell some stories—many of us in this line of work could—but Phil is one-of-a-kind.

If you love hockey and good stories—and if you love fictional characters who were actually very much nonfiction characters—this is the book for you. If you elect to not take this adventure, I can only say one thing to you: shame on you for six weeks.

Now, enjoy the book.

—Mike Lange
Pittsburgh Penguins radio play-by-play broadcaster

CHAPTER 1
BEGIN AT THE BEGINNING

It was early on the morning of May 26, 1991. I was drunk, happy, overwhelmed, tired, and in need of a ride.

A few hours earlier, we had won the Stanley Cup in Minnesota. We were greeted by 40,000 fans at the airport and, frankly, the party got a little out of control.

My future wife, Julie, and I were on the parkway hitchhiking for a ride home. Back then, that's how we Ubered. We got that ride and got home safely, because that's the kind of town Pittsburgh is. It's not a city. It's a town. And it's my town.

I've lived the life and then some, but through all the ups and downs, being a member of the Penguins organization and calling Pittsburgh my home always brought out the best in me.

To this day, it still does. It was truly a pleasure to play on one of the greatest hockey teams ever assembled. I played with Mario Lemieux, the greatest hockey player in history. Kevin "Artie" Stevens. Jaromir Jagr. Ron Francis. Paul Coffey. Larry Murphy. Ulf Samuelsson. Joey Mullen. Tom Barrasso. Rick Tocchet. Mark Recchi. Bryan Trottier. We were coached by Bob Johnson and Scotty Bowman. Craig Patrick was our general manger. It's a Hall of Fame wing, basically.

We weren't just a great hockey team, either. We had personality. We lived large. We worked hard and played harder. We were as entertaining off the ice as we were on the ice, and I don't think we ever played a game that could have been considered boring. We were a bunch of alpha males, and believe me when I tell you that there's never been a Stanley Cup team that wasn't equipped with a bunch of alpha males. No way, no how. We were different, though. We were a bunch of renegades. We had coaches fired when it was necessary. We played defense at our own risk. Don't think for one second, though, that we didn't want to win. Did we ever. We won the Cup two years in a row, and the only thing that stopped us from winning four or five straight was Mario's health and the financial reality of the time. We just couldn't keep that team together because, at that time, the money wasn't in Pittsburgh. That doesn't mean, however, that we weren't an all-time great team. If there's a heaven and they let you play hockey there, I'll put the early '90s Penguins against any team that ever lived, and we'll beat their asses.

My life peaked in the early '90s in many ways, being a role player on a team that truly did change the game. We were so good and so unstoppable offensively that we damn near shut down the game later that decade. And no, I'm not kidding. The neutral zone trap and teams generally focusing on defense above all else was a direct result of what we were doing to the league.

You're going to read about all of those times, the good, the bad, the ugly, and the surreal, all through my eyes.

But my journey began a long way from that early morning on the parkway.

I grew up just outside of Boston, in Chelmsford, Massachusetts, with my parents and two brothers.

When I was three years old, a friend of my father's took me to a public ice skating rink. Later that day, the friend told my dad something that would play a pretty important role in my life.

"Your kid is unbelievable. You might want to get him a pair of skates."

Just like that, my life in the wild, wonderful world of hockey began.

The house I grew up in was just a little ranch house with a 20-foot driveway. My dad would hose the driveway down and turn it into a miniature ice rink. It didn't take much in those Boston winters in the 1960s, so my driveway was my own personal heaven as a little one. Even when I'd start going to ice rinks on a more regular basis at that age, I was in love. I didn't know how to stop yet, so I'd just go head first right into the boards, check my faculties, brush myself off, and skate some more. You can't teach that. You can't invent that. You're born with that joy for the game or you're not. Plain and simple. I was born with it.

A few years later, we moved into a bigger house. At that time, I had my own 20-by-40 rink in my back yard. For the first time in my life, I was in love. My parents actually had to have spotlights installed in the back yard, because you literally couldn't get me off the ice. I was obsessed. It didn't matter what time of day or night it was, I was out there. When I was a kid, I literally slept with my equipment on. I would have slept with my skates on if my mom let me. All I really cared about was the game. I started playing organized hockey. Back in those days, games were so early because ice time wasn't easy to obtain. I didn't care what time the games were played. If it was a 4:00 AM puck drop, hell, I'd have been ready to go. Even now, in my fifties, I still possess that same insatiable love for the game of hockey. I don't know why or where it came from. I didn't grow up in a hockey family. I never saw my dad in a pair of skates. To the best of my knowledge, no one played hockey in my entire extended family. My dad played football and baseball at Boston College, so I definitely had some athletic genes in my family. But the love for the game of ice hockey was all my own, and it was a love that has never faded.

By the time I was at the Peewee level, I knew I was good. I was starting to really excel. It's said that professional athletes are usually, though not always, pretty easy to identify in childhood. No question, I was ahead of most kids my age, and I was playing in Boston, which isn't exactly novice hockey country.

As my hockey ability started to blossom, so too did the physical abuse I received from my father, Richard Bourque. I guess you could say I developed a love-hate relationship with hockey as a result.

My dad did some good things for me, no question. He had that ice rink built for me. And money was tight for long stretches of time. I don't know how he afforded to keep me playing on all these different teams, because I was often playing for expensive teams, more than one at a time. I think he remortgaged the house a couple of times. Seriously. So, that was appreciated.

However, it doesn't make up for the things he did to me as a child.

Simply put, if I had a bad game, my dad would beat the shit out of me. The abuse was vicious. He was an arrogant prick, born with a silver spoon in his mouth in Boston. He just literally didn't have a soft side to him. Not in the least. But he knew how to make people like him. He was real gabby, a salesman in downtown Boston. If anyone out there has ever lived on strict commission, you know how incredibly stressful and difficult that can be. You literally don't know what your next check will be, so you fight your ass off every day of your life. I will say for my dad that his work ethic was unsurpassed by anything I've ever witnessed in my life. And he was good at his job, no doubt. The guy could sell ice to an Eskimo. But he was also an intolerable bully at every stage of my childhood. He wasn't always very nice to my mom, and he treated me like absolute shit.

At some point, he became utterly obsessed with my hockey career and utterly obsessed with me being the best. I'm all for pushing your kids to be as good as they can be, but his intense interest in me being the best youth hockey player in Boston was beyond strange. If I had a bad game, or even had a bad moment in a game, I would generally fall victim. And again, this wasn't when I was 18. I was much younger when these incidents would take place. I'd have a rough game and, when I got home, I'd go to my bedroom. Then, he would wait for me. When I walked out of my bedroom, right after opening the door, he would sucker punch me right in

13

the face. He'd slap me around with an open hand, slaps, punches, all of it. The worst beatings involved his belt. If I had a really bad game, he'd make me drop my pants and he'd whip the hell out of my ass with his belt. He'd just whip me over and over. I'd bend over on my bed and he would just relentlessly crack me with that belt. I can still feel it, can still hear the noise it made. The beatings generally depended on how badly I played. If I had some great game, it wouldn't happen. If I had a so-so game, I'd receive some abuse. But if I had a really bad game, I knew I was getting my ass kicked when I got home. Talk about pressure to play well.

So, as a young man, I was living a big contradiction. Hockey was really the only thing that made me feel good, my only joy. As far as I'm concerned, it's the greatest game in the world, and I realized this at a very young age. I had a real talent for it and passion to match. That's a great thing, right? But damn, I learned to hate hockey, too. The game sometimes led me down a horrible path, as I would endure one beating after another. As a result, I was dealing with a lot of turbulence. I put enough pressure on myself to play well to begin with, but fearing for your health is a different kind of pressure, and one I lived with daily as a child.

Maybe dealing with that kind of pressure prepared me for life as a hockey player down the road, in a sick kind of way. See, I liked being nervous before games. Hell, I still get nervous before games when I'm in the broadcast booth. I've always liked that pit in my stomach. I always liked playoff games a little more than regular season games, and I don't think all players are wired quite like that. Some are, sure. But not all of them. I was like that. Game Sevens were my personal favorites. The more pressure, the better I played and the more I enjoyed it. When you deal with the kind of pressure I dealt with as a kid, the pressure of a hockey game is different, and I don't think it affects you as negatively as it might otherwise. To say the least, that element of my childhood was pretty bizarre. And the funny thing is, the rest of my family life was really good. I get along well with my brothers to this day. I don't see them as often as I'd like, but we have a good relationship. My mother is the sweetest woman on Earth. But dealing with my dad as a child was something that I wouldn't wish on anyone. Did it toughen me up? Sure, I guess it did. What kind of a way is that to develop toughness, though? It was truly horrible.

Growing up in Boston during that time made you mature pretty quickly on the ice rink. Games were tough. Players were good. By the time I was a snot-nosed 14-year-old, I was playing Junior A hockey against guys who were 17 to 19. These guys were drinking. They were driving to games. Sometimes they were drinking and driving to games. Here I am, 14 years old. Chris Nilan was in that league, some other really good, tough players. My God, did I have to grow up quickly to function in that league, but it made me a better player, I promise you that.

I finally played high school hockey my senior year. It wasn't real fashionable for the best players to play on their high school teams back then and, truth be told, it still isn't. But we actually had some good players at that point in time, so I played my final year. The coaches and other players knew I was good and that I could help. We made it all the way to the state quarterfinals that year and in our final game we had a chance to play in Boston Garden. Wow. Little thrills like that—okay, it was a big thrill—just whet my appetite more and more. From the time I was a kid, it was my dream to play in the NHL and to play for the Boston Bruins. To get a chance to play on that ice surface at 17? It was a pretty big moment in my life, no doubt about it.

Luckily, there was my mom. She always gave me nothing but love and encouragement, the nicest human being on earth. What an amazing woman. I still visit her in Boston as often as I can. She is a simple woman, grew up on a farm in Massachusetts. And what an amazing mom she was. She wasn't a party animal, but she never stopped me from being one.

As you might imagine, I rather enjoyed having a good time in my youth. I have many memories of drinking with my high school buddies. I'd be 16, 17 years old, and my friends and I would be having a good time. We'd end up back at my house at midnight. My mom would always come downstairs, look at us, and say, "You need to be quiet. Don't wake up your father. Now let me fix you something to eat."

So, in a matter of minutes, we'd have a big stack of pancakes, scrambled eggs, and toast looking us right in the eye. That was my mom. Everyone loved Mrs. B. My friends all adored her, as did I. And I needed the love that she provided. Growing up around my dad, you know, it was rough. Really rough. My mom loved me and gave me the foundation I needed to be a good person and to someday be a good dad.

My parents finally divorced, many years later. My mom confided in me and my brothers that she was thinking about herself. I told her that I endorsed that decision. My dad found out about this and we had a huge, huge falling out. I had witnessed, firsthand, the way he had treated her over the years. I was very much in favor of the divorce, and I told him that. We had a face-to-face chat. What he said, I'll never forget.

"I disown you as my son," he said.

Can you believe that? All the shit he had put me through, and I always kept my mouth shut, never got in trouble, always just took it. And he was disowning me as his son.

I didn't hesitate to respond.

"Fuck you."

I didn't talk with him again for 10 years.

Over the next couple of years, he would write me probably 20 letters. He called me 50 times. I didn't read one of those letters, nor did I answer one of those phone calls. The way he had treated me, and the way he had treated my beloved mother, it was too much for me to handle. He didn't deserve my love or my respect.

So yeah, my childhood wasn't all bad, but it certainly had its moments. By the time 1980 rolled around, I was graduating high school and my childhood was coming to an end. I had myself a very big decision to make.

Most kids in the New England area go on to play college hockey. It's just what you do. There are Boston College, B.U., and so many other outstanding schools for hockey. My grades were fine and I was a really good player. The natural course of action would have been to stay local and do the college hockey thing.

But the fact of the matter is, I wanted—no, make that I needed—to get as far away from my dad as I possibly could. I was looking for the path away from him and to the National Hockey League. It wasn't easy, any of it. Figuring out what you want to do with your life at that age, in those circumstances, is a horribly difficult thing. Remember what life was like for you at 17? You probably weren't all that ready to make real-world decisions because you were still a kid. Trust me, that's exactly how I felt. Back then, Americans made it to the NHL, but certainly not with the same frequency that you see today. People would look at you like you were crazy if you said you were going to play in the NHL one day. So what were you going to do? Just go to college anyway and get an education? Find a labor job and live a tough life where at least you had enough money to get by? Or pursue the hockey dream?

Meanwhile, all I could think about was getting the hell away from my father, and as soon as possible. I hated the idea of leaving my mom and my hometown, but sometimes the self-preservation instinct kicks in. The beatings started when I was young, and they didn't stop into my teenage years. It was still happening a good bit. He was a big, strong man and I dealt with so much. I was just about done. All I could think about was finding a way out of Boston that could still help me get to the NHL.

Life is sometimes all about taking advantage of the breaks that you receive, however. And I was about to get one of the biggest breaks of my life.

CHAPTER 2
THE EASIEST DECISION

We lost the high school game in Boston Garden, but I played well. I was pretty preoccupied with the surroundings and not much else. Little did I know, however, that someone was watching me play, someone who was a big deal.

Gentleman Jean Ratelle, a Hockey Hall of Famer who was finishing up his career with the Bruins during the 1979–80 season, was watching me play with a mutual friend of my family's. At this point, I was still strictly a defenseman, and I played a really good game. Skating was my game. I could really fly.

The next thing I know, Gentleman Jean is sitting in my living room. Talk about surreal.

Bob Tindel was a scout with the Bruins and a family friend. They're both sitting there in my freaking living room. I did my best to stay calm, but it wasn't easy. Trust me. It wasn't easy at all. This is basically like if Brian Dumoulin was watching the WPIAL championships at PPG Paints Arena, was impressed with some defenseman from New Kensington, and drove to his house to talk with him about his career the next day. Stuff like this just doesn't happen very often.

They both told me that I was good. Really good. They thought I could potentially have a career as an NHL player. I was already confident in myself, but if I ever needed more belief, my God, there it was. Jean looked at me and said, "What do you want to do with your career? You're a good hockey player. I can help you."

Now, my dad wanted me to get a scholarship in college and get a job. I wanted to play pro hockey. Two different things. And honestly, I wanted to get the hell away from the idea of college or of being in Boston. So, Jean said he knows a guy who can help. Jim Morrison, who played with the Penguins, was the coach of a junior hockey team in Kingston, Ontario. He told me he could get me a tryout that summer in Kingston, before the season started. That's all I needed to hear. They had certain rules, mind you. I was allowed to go try out with Kingston during a 48-hour window and, if I left at that point, I could still retain my amateur eligibility. You must understand that very, very few Americans had done anything like that at that point. Year later, Pittsburgh kids like Brandon Saad and Vince Trocheck went the Ontario Hockey League route. But we're talking 1980 here. It was almost 40 years ago, and it was pretty much a Canadian-only league at that time. Still, I wasn't thinking twice about this offer. I accepted immediately.

At this point in time, I was really starting to believe in myself and in hockey as my future. The way I played in the Boston Garden, and how comfortable I felt, made a huge impression on me. Gentleman Jean's seemingly sincere, glowing review of my game was an even bigger deal. Something else happened that year, too. A few months earlier, Herb Brooks and Team USA pulled off the Miracle on Ice at the Olympics in Lake Placid, defeating the Soviet Union in the most important hockey game ever played. For any young American hockey player, that game was an enormous deal. At that point, hockey was basically a fringe sport in the United States. Baseball and football were kings at that time, and even though hockey was huge where I grew up, the Celtics had just drafted a kid named Larry Bird and basketball was about to receive quite a boon. Hockey was pretty much considered a sport that was dominated by Canadians and Europeans. Truth to be told, that's exactly what hockey was at that point. Then along came Herb and a fast, gritty bunch of Americans, and everything changed. What I noticed immediately following the Olympics was that, with all due respect to Al Michaels, it wasn't really a miracle at all. In fact, many players on that team turned pro after the Olympics and turned into very good NHL players. If that team had somehow defeated the mighty Russians in a fluke game, it still would have been a big deal. Herb still would have been a god. We'd still brag about that game from now until the end of time.

That so many of those guys—Neal Broten, Mike Ramsey, Kenny Morrow, on and on—immediately became good NHL players told me something. *If they can do it, so can I.*

Suddenly, hockey wasn't just a sport for being north of the border or across the ocean. It was America's game too. The sense of pride many people talk about when it comes to that game is totally legitimate. Afer that game, as an American hockey player, my chest felt a little bit bigger. Those guys will always have a special place in my heart for what they did under Herb. They made everyone from my generation believe a little bit more.

So, August arrives. I make my way to Kingston. It's a beautiful city, if you've never been there. I liked it because it was a nice place, the girls were pretty, and it was hundreds of miles from Boston. Good combination.

Over the course of two days—remember, the 48-hour rule—I participated in a number of scrimmages. Kingston, at that time, had a good team and had seven players who would go on to play in the NHL. Some of them were on the ice during the scrimmages, but I didn't feel out of place in the least.

Coach Morrison called me into his office after the second day of the workouts.

"I thought you were great," he said.

He asked me what I wanted to do. A little bit of American confidence then erupted out of me.

"Here's what I want," I said. "I want you to write down the names of the players who were out there today that have already been drafted."

He pulled out a pen and a piece of paper and wrote down five or six names. He then slid the piece of paper to me. I took a look at the paper.

"I'm as good as if not better than every guy on this list," I said.

Then I pushed the piece of paper back to him. I told him that I wanted to stay.

His response?

"That's good enough for me. I need you to call your parents and tell them you're not coming home."

I haven't really been home since.

He gave me $300 and told me to buy whatever clothes and toiletries that I required. Not long after that, he found me a family to live with. All I had to do was tell my parents to send my stuff and to let them know I wasn't coming home. It's funny, as a professional athlete—or in this case, as an aspiring professional athlete—you have so many damn decisions to make. The decisions seemingly never stop. When you're 18, you're not necessarily equipped to make all the right decisions and, believe me when I tell you, I made some bad ones along the way. But that August day in Kingston, hell, that was the easiest decision I ever had to make in my life. Come on. Not only was I getting away from my dad, but I was truly getting an opportunity to play hockey at a high level in a nice town. I couldn't have been happier, and the choice couldn't have been easier.

I had just graduated high school in June, and by the end of August, I'm living with a family I don't know and some hotshot named Bernie Nicholls. Bernie was Kingston's star and was a hell of a player. He'd later go on to become an impact player at the NHL level. His girlfriend at the time was Miss Teen Ontario, of all things. Good times for Bernie.

The family I lived with owned two seasonal businesses. In the summer, they ran a drive-in theater. In the winter, they sold fur coats. The first year I lived there, they wanted to promote this big Christmas sale, so they had Bernie and me pose for ads in the *Kingston Whig-Standard* newspaper. As a perk, we were allowed to keep the fur coats. For the rest of the season, Bernie and I showed up at every junior hockey game wearing fur coats. His was a full-length coyote. Mine was a full-length beaver. What a couple of clowns we must have looked like. I can't even imagine how ridiculous we looked, but come on; we were just kids and we weren't about to turn down that deal.

I even got serious with a girl in Kingston. Bernie and his girlfriend came out with me one time and she brought a friend. Her name was Gundie. She was a German girl with blonde hair. Oh yeah. I was in business. She was gorgeous, and we really hit it off quite nicely while I was in Kingston. It was the perfect junior hockey league romance. When I think back to my time in Kingston, I smile. I grew up a lot as a person during those two seasons, and I developed into a pretty damn good hockey player. Nowadays, you can make arguments between NCAA Hockey and the Canadian Hockey League. Back then, it was no contest. Playing in Kingston absolutely elevated my level of play and by a pretty substantial margin.

After my second season in Kingston, I was draft eligible. I hired an agent by the name of Ivan Prud'homme. He was a nobody, to be honest. Hell, I think I was his only client. Seriously. He had a very thick French accent, a heavy-set guy. He was quite the bullshit artist. I didn't really think I'd be drafted in the first three rounds, but at any time after that, I was certain I would be selected. There were 12 rounds in the draft back then, and there was no doubt in my mind someone would give me a look. Maybe my hometown Bruins. Whoever. I really didn't care.

After my second season in Kingston, I was living back at home in Boston and working at a gas station. It was a full-service station. The draft was held on a Saturday in Montreal, but I was still back at home, working that day, in fact. Ivan had the phone number at the gas station and he kept calling throughout the day. I'd be pumping someone's gas when my boss would holler for me to come inside.

"Your agent's calling," he said. "Maybe you were drafted."
Or maybe not. "I just talked with a team," he'd say. "They're
going to take you in this round."
It would repeat itself time and time again in the fourth and
fifth rounds. Finally, it got to the sixth round. Ivan calls me again.
"I just talked with the Quebec Nordiques," he said. "They're
going to take you in that round."
That was the last time I ever heard from Ivan. The Nordiques
didn't draft me, of course. Nobody drafted me, in fact. I was absolutely devastated. I knew I wasn't going in the top three rounds, but
come the hell on. I could really fly and I was pretty sound defensively, too. The game had changed in the previous 15 years because
of guys like Bobby Orr and the emerging Paul Coffey. No, I wasn't
anywhere close to their level. But defensemen who played in the
offensive zone were suddenly a hot commodity, and I had proven
that I was effective in that role against many NHL draft picks in
Kingston. I wasn't lying to Coach Morrison when I told him I was
better than those guys on the sheet of paper. I really meant it and
believe I proved during the next two seasons that I was indeed on
their respective levels. Now I wasn't even going to get drafted? How
could this even be possible? I was more upset than you could possibly imagine and decided to part ways with Ivan. Do I think he was
lying to me? Nah, I'm sure he did talk with some NHL teams about
me. I know that they knew who I was. I'm sure some of them gave
him the courtesy answer and said they'd be happy to select me, blah,
blah, blah. I couldn't shake the feeling that he was embellishing, that
he was basically bullshitting me. So I told him I no longer wanted
to be represented by him and that our relationship was through. I
never spoke with him again.

The next morning represented a real crossroads in my life. We've
all been there, right? There are important moments in your life, those

moments you'll remember clear as day when you're old. The next morning was one such moment for me. This wasn't 2019. There was no Internet to speak of. Back then, we got our news from the newspaper. On that next morning, the *Boston Globe* was in my hands and I was shaking I was so angry. I've never seen a newspaper do this before or since, but on that day, the *Globe* printed a full page insert that included the name of every player selected in the 1982 NHL Entry Draft. Full names. Junior teams. Hometown. Position. The whole goddamn nine yards. I could have just crumpled up that newspaper and thrown it away. Moved on with my life. Considered going to college or looking for a job. I could have given up. It's bad enough that I wasn't drafted, but to see all those other names in the newspaper? To have it publicized like that? It was awful. It would be like losing the girl of your dreams to some asshole and then seeing it published for the whole world to read about the next day. That's how much I cared.

I didn't crumple that newspaper up. I didn't throw it away. Instead, I let it inspire me, one day at a time. I taped it to the mirror on my dresser. I found a black Sharpie and wrote on top of the page, "Where are you?"

Every morning, I'd look at it. And I wouldn't just glance at it. I'd stare at it. I'd feel that pain. It made every single workout that much more important for me. I worked my ass off that summer, hoping I was going to get a phone call from a team that would invite me to training camp. You'll never know how hard it pushed me. When you don't get drafted, that's usually pretty much it. The odds of making it to the NHL when you aren't drafted are pretty horrendous, especially back then. But something told me not to give up. I've never been so hungry for something as I was to make it to the NHL, so I kept working and trying to will that phone to ring.

A month later, I received two phone calls, one from the Boston Bruins and another from the Pittsburgh Penguins. They both invited me to training camp.

The choice was an easy one. For one, I was a little pissed that the Bruins didn't draft me. I was from right around the corner. They had to have known who I was. Then there was the fact that I wanted nothing to do with being in Boston, because I rather enjoyed those two years away from my dad. There was another important item that can't be ignored. When you're in that position, when you don't get drafted and you know that most people consider you a long shot to ever make the NHL, you don't want to play for a good team. The Bruins weren't quite as good as they were when they had Bobby Orr and Phil Esposito a decade earlier, but they were still something of a powerhouse and I figured that breaking into that organization was always going to be a chore. Pittsburgh, though? The team actually had made the playoffs the year before and nearly upset the Islanders in the first round. But they had a bunch of older guys on that team, players like Rick Kehoe. They had a few good, established veterans, like Randy Carlyle, but I had done my homework. They didn't have any good, young players in their system at all. They had never won anything. They weren't a good team at all and it seemed like it would be a hell of a lot easier to catch a break with the Penguins.

So I chose Pittsburgh without ever thinking twice. I borrowed my mom's 1978 Mercury Cougar and drove from Boston to Pittsburgh. I still remember that drive in September 1982, driving through the tunnels for the first time, seeing the skyline of Pittsburgh explode before me. It was another one of those moments in your life that you'll never forget. At that very moment, to be honest with you, I felt as though I had arrived. I was home.

You always hear these things about Pittsburgh when you're a kid, that it's not a nice place, that it's nothing but smoke. Maybe it was like that once upon a time, but when I saw it for the first time, it wasn't like that at all. It was the most beautiful thing I had ever seen. From my first moment there, I was comfortable and I knew that I was about to embark on a special time in my life.

They put me up in a hotel for my first few nights in Pittsburgh. They had to give us physicals and things of that nature. Then, we'd be having training camp at the War Memorial in Johnstown, Pennsylvania. That's right, the place where they had filmed *Slap Shot* five years earlier. Hockey pretty much was like *Slap Shot* back then and I very easily could have been a character from that movie.

I was such a rebel in those days. All I did was live on the edge. It never stopped with me and, go figure, it happened on my very first night in the 'Burgh. They gave me a roommate by the name of Gary Conn. He was a New England guy, played college hockey in New Hampshire. So that's why they put us together. So we're just hanging out on the first night and he says to me, "Hey, I hear the University of Pittsburgh is a pretty good school. Want to check it out?"

What that meant was, "Let's try to get lucky with some college girls."

So that's what we proceeded to do. What a night that was. On my first night in Pittsburgh, I ended up in a frat house at 3 a.m. at the University of Pittsburgh. I was doing funnel shots all night and didn't know where the hell I was by the end of the night. By the grace of God, I made it back to my hotel in one piece.

Luckily I got the fun out of my system quickly, because the next morning, we took a bus to Johnston for the most important few weeks of my life. I had to let it fly at training camp. What other choice did I have? Seriously, this was it. I wasn't drafted. You had better be willing to do everything at camp to get noticed when you're in the situation I was in. Fight. Skate your ass off. Listen to everything the coaches say. You name it, that's what I had to do.

Training camps back then were fucking scary. It wasn't just about playing hockey. There was a macho element to it all. I wasn't afraid of it, but it wasn't exactly what you'd consider a leisurely experience either.

And the thing was, I didn't have a Plan B. Basically, it was get a contract, or you're probably fucked for the rest of your life. That was my mentality and it probably wasn't wrong. I either got a contract or I would have to drag my ass back to Boston, look my dad in the eye, and tell him I failed. Talk about things I didn't want to do.

I had the camp of my life. I couldn't really have played any better. I busted my ass every single day and, as 20-year-old nobody who wasn't drafted, I almost made the team. I was the last person cut, in fact. But the news wasn't all bad.

I got called into Baz Bastien's office. He was the general manager of the Penguins. As fate would have it, he was killed in a car accident about six months later and would be replaced by Eddie Johnston, who was the Penguins' coach at the time. Baz had this little corner office in the War Memorial.

"Kid, you had a great camp," he said. "I'd like to sign you to a two-year deal. Here's how it works. You're going to [AHL] Baltimore now. If you get called up to Pittsburgh, you'll be making $60,000 a year. In Baltimore, you'll be making $18,500 per year to play in the American League."

Then he paused. This scared the shit out of me. I was afraid he was reconsidering what he had just said. For just a moment, my heart totally sunk to my damn feet. Then, he said this: "You know, I really like you, kid. So, I'm going to give you a $5,000 signing bonus."

I truly couldn't believe what I had just been told. Are you fucking kidding me? I got my contract, they're giving me a two-year deal, which means I have a chance to play in the NHL soon, and they're giving me an extra $5,000 just to sign this deal? I was totally in shock.

Plus, it's not like Baltimore was Siberia. It was a big city. It wasn't all that far from my home in Boston, it was only four hours away from Pittsburgh and an hour away from Washington D.C. if I felt like having some fun. Of course I would have loved making my way from where I was to the NHL all in one swoop. And I damn near did. But still, I had made an incredible amount of progress in a very, very short period of time. Only three months earlier, I had dealt with the indignity of not being drafted when I knew damn well I deserved to have my name called. Talk about something that's tough to swallow. But I did things the right way the whole time. I didn't pout. I didn't give up. I just put my head down and worked my ass off, harder than I'd ever worked for anything in my entire life. I'd gotten a taste of what life was going to be like in the National Hockey League. I'd gotten real money and was going to be making a living playing this game. My dream of playing in the NHL was alive and well.

I didn't know how long it was going to take to establish myself at the NHL level, but I was on my way. You're damn right I was.

CHAPTER 3
WELCOME
TO THE NHL

Life in Baltimore wasn't horrible at all. The Colts were still there, the Orioles were a World Series team and, in general, I just thought it was a cool city and a fine sports town. And another thing: we played before packed houses every single night. It was a hell of a good hockey town, a surprisingly good one. I don't think of hockey when I think of Maryland, but they really got behind us. We had this little ring of fire thing that we skated through when we took the ice. The people were so into it. If you were going to be relegated to the minor leagues, this wasn't the worst place to be.

But I had some funny shit happen to me in Baltimore. More to the point, I got arrested. Twice. Talk about some fluke shit, though. Check out what happened.

My first season there was the 1982–83 campaign. We had a really good team, and some future teammates in Pittsburgh played there, people like Rod Buskus and Dave Hannan, among others. Mitch Lamoureux had a big season, putting up 57 goals. He also needed to put up some bail money because of a little incident.

Mitch and I were out at a bar one evening and I was actually the designated driver. I didn't have a drink in my system, in fact. Mitch, on the other hand, was absolutely shitfaced. You'll recall that I was given that $5,000 signing bonus. With that money, in characteristic fashion, I figured the best thing to do was to buy a Corvette. Seems reasonable, right? The only problem with Corvettes is that they're really low to the ground. So, like I said, Mitch had absorbed perhaps one too many beverages. I was literally trying to help him get into the Corvette, but he was really struggling. I then walked over to give him a hand. However, as I'm trying to put Mitch into the car, I notice him make eye contact with another guy. Oh shit.

He sees some guy looking at us and looking at the car. Mitch looks at him and says, "What the fuck are you looking at?"

I said, "Mitch, let it go, buddy. Come on. Let's get out of here." But Mitch was really liquored up and kept letting him hear it. Mitch then pushed me away and got in this guy's face. They start pushing each other. That's the last thing I remember, to be honest. I don't think I've ever been at the wrong place at the wrong time more than at that particular moment. I shit you not, within 30 seconds of them shoving each other, I was in handcuffs. Really. I remember saying out loud, "What the fuck just happened?"

Well, here's what happened. The guy Mitch was having words with was a fucking undercover cop. Yeah. Apparently we disrupted a drug bust that was underway, and that didn't go over so well. Next thing I know, I'm sitting in jail for assaulting a police officer. It's not so easy to get out of that accusation, right? It made all the newspapers. It was on the news. It was everywhere at the time, and I was convinced that it marked the end of my hockey career. Convinced. I was an undrafted nobody at the time. Why in the hell would the Penguins keep someone like me around? There was no doubt in my mind that they were going to release me, which probably would have been worse than not getting that contract in the first place. The Penguins, however, never really seemed to give a shit. No one ever said anything to me. Not one word about it.

One year later, it happened again. I was once again the innocent bystander. If I was going to get arrested, I could have at least done something that was moderately badass. But nah, that didn't exactly work out.

This time, I'm literally just waiting to get into a bar. I'm standing in a line waiting to get in. That's it. I'm not doing anything else. I'm not the least bit intoxicated. A lot of guys on the team were going to the same bar and our assistant equipment manager happens to see me. "Hey Bourquey! Hey Bourquey!"

The guy was so happy to see me that he kind of jumped on me and knocked me over. I guess the two of us laying on the ground made a bit of a scene, but once again, I wasn't really expecting to feel handcuffs on my wrists. A few seconds later, though, and those damn handcuffs were back.

Drunk and disorderly conduct. Get the fuck out of here. But yeah, it happened. This time, I figured, I'm totally screwed. It's not a big deal to get arrested that first time, maybe. The second arrest in as many years almost surely indicates that you're a bad apple. I knew the release was coming. I just knew it. I was mentally prepared for it.

Once again, it never happened. I never heard a word from the Penguins about anything. I knew they knew. It was on the news. It wasn't a secret. They either trusted the hell out of me for they just didn't give a shit. I'm not really sure which it was, but I'm surely grateful about it.

Of course, maybe the timing had something to do with it, also. The second arrest came in the 1983–84 season, and I actually started the season at the NHL level. I played in my first NHL game on October 4, 1983. One year earlier, on October 4, 1982, I had signed my first NHL contract. I was proud of the progress I made and I damn near scored on my first NHL shot. In the first period against the Blues, I had goalie Mike Liut beaten but rang a shot off the crossbar. We lost 5–3, but I wasn't in any position to complain. It was my first taste of life in the NHL, and I'll never forget it. The Blues played in the Checker Dome at the time, a real bandbox if ever there has been one. I remember ringing that one off the cross bar, but other than that, I don't have any particular recollections from that game. It's all a total blur, to be honest. I just know that it was a good thing, the start of something for me. I played in the first five games that season before again playing a season in Baltimore, but getting that taste of life in the NHL, and of life in Pittsburgh, was a big deal to me.

The 1983–84 Penguins are somewhat infamous, of course. For good reason. Holy shit were we bad. In fact, after I was sent back to Baltimore, guys on the team talked about how we would have beaten the Penguins in a game. And we would have. So why wasn't I in the NHL? It would be easy for me to tell you, "Because they didn't want any good players in Pittsburgh that season."

It's not that simple, though. See, they didn't want any good players in Pittsburgh. Eddie Johnston, the new general manager, was no idiot. He had heard of the phenom from Montreal named Mario Lemieux. Of course the Penguins tanked that season. It's no secret. Funny thing is, I knew I wasn't ready to be in the NHL just yet. Oh, I wanted to be. But it takes time. It wasn't easy to march into that league as a kid and make it all work. For most of us, it takes time, especially while laying defense. All things considered, I think I was pretty patient during this time. Still, there were some teammates in Baltimore who were legitimately pissed off that they weren't called up to the big time, and, truth be told, I felt bad for many of them. They were ready to play in the NHL. We had some really good players in Baltimore and the Penguins were playing to lose because of some guy named Mario Lemieux from Montreal.

Had we heard about Mario? Yeah, of course. But at that time, I hadn't seen any video or anything like that. He was just a rumor. A big, beautiful rumor. Sometimes phenoms work out and sometimes they don't. The feeling on the team was, "For all you know, he's not going to be any good, so let's just play for ourselves."

I remember all the things I heard about Mario. That he was the savior, shit like that. Heck, I hoped he was, but I wasn't really buying it. Every time his name would come up during the 1983–84 season, you heard about how he was going to save the Penguins. Although that was one of the worst teams in NHL history, I can say that it wasn't easy being on that team. No one wants to be part of a historically bad team or to be part of a tank job. Even though it wasn't a good team, there was still some legitimate pride there. A lot of it had to be swallowed during that season.

Best stat from that season? Mike Bullard scored 51 goals for the Penguins that year, and not one of them was a game-winner. Seriously. That's how bad it was. That's all you have to know about how truly awful that edition of the Penguins was.

By the 1984–85 season, I was eager to prove that I belonged. Baltimore was great, but enough of that shit. I wanted to make real money playing for the team that drafted me. Gone were the days of having training camp in Johnstown. It was now a Pittsburgh thing. We held our practices at the Mt. Lebanon Arena, and everything was so damn different because of Mario. When that camp started, people were literally 10-deep to get a glimpse of him. That's how big a deal he was. In my first two training camps with the Penguins, I'd estimate there were about 10 fans in attendance, and I'm willing to bet that five of them knew nothing about the sport, and the other five were probably homeless.

Mario certainly brought a circuslike atmosphere to practice every day.

In drills during that camp, I had finally had enough. I was going to take a run at the new kid, I decided. I don't give a shit if he's a phenom. So, we're playing Mario's team in this scrimmage. Throwing hip checks was a particular specialty of mine. So, Mario's skating with the puck through the middle of the ice, and oh baby did I have him lined up. I'm skating up to absolutely bury him, and then, at the last second, he does this insanely ridiculous 360-degree spin. It's something I've only ever seen Sidney Crosby do before. He left me in the dust, laying there on the ice like a fool.

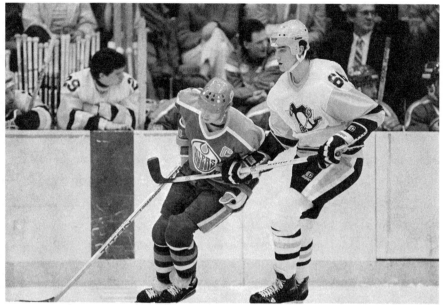

Mario Lemieux was billed as the savior of the Penguins. I'd say he lived up to the hype. (AP Images)

I thought to myself, *Oh my God. Oh my God. He really is different. He really is going to be a superstar. He really is one of those guys.*

Let me tell you, it didn't a whole lot of research on my part. I only needed to see Mario skate once or twice and I realized exactly what I was witnessing. It was that easy, really.

I felt bad for Mario during camp. At first, anyway. He was really, really shy, for one thing, and he was a young kid in a new city, younger than I ever was. That can be a difficult thing to deal with. Plus, there was the language barrier. It would take a lot of hard work for Mario to get comfortable speaking English, but he finally did.

So, imagine what Mario was dealing with. He didn't speak very good English. He was almost painfully shy. Idiots like me were taking runs at him. There was almost no talent in Pittsburgh for Mario to work with. The Penguins were counting on him to lift them out of last place every night.

That pretty much sums it up. The pressure on him to lift the Penguins was immense.

It's funny, though. Mario had all these things working against him and, like I said, he was just so shy and introverted by nature. But, I have to say, I always knew Mario was going to lead us to greatness. Always. And it's not just because of the talent I witnessed in training camp, even though it was a dazzling display the likes of which I'll never see again.

Nah, I knew the Penguins had a true superstar in Mario by the way he carried himself. There was something totally royal, totally regal, about Mario and the way he carried himself. He had this little swagger in the way he walked. He wasn't cocky. He wasn't arrogant. But he also knew that he was better than anybody in that locker room and knew after a few years he would be perhaps the greatest hockey player who ever lived. I'm telling you, something in the way he walked was just different. His body language was that of a veteran player, someone who was very sure of himself.

Yeah, that was the biggest thing with Mario. To this day, I've never seen another hockey player who was that sure of himself. I've never seen anything like it at all, to be honest with you. Even though he was just 18 at the time, there was something undeniably different about Mario. Sometimes I used to think that he was well aware that he was put on this earth to conquer the game of hockey, and that he was okay with that.

Everything about his genius was on display during that training camp. The goal-scoring ability, the hard shot, the vision, the breakaway artistry, the stick handling. To witness it firsthand during training camp was quite a pleasure. I'm glad to say I was on the ice during that training camp.

Getting to see the Mario Show up close and personal was one hell of a thrill. There was only one problem: I wanted to see it every night, not once a month, not just every summer during camp. I was sent back down to Baltimore again, and this one really hurt. You see, I immediately realized when I saw Mario in that first training camp that, eventually, this was going to be a special hockey team. All I wanted was to be a part of it.

But I had a long way to go.

CHAPTER 4

FINALLY
MAKING IT,
ALYSSA MILANO,
AND SO MUCH
MORE

Things changed after seeing the Mario Show in training camp. I didn't make the team that year, so I had to sit in Baltimore and read the box scores the next day. The 1984–85 Penguins were pretty bad, but Mario was putting up 100 points surrounded by those guys, which was no small feat.

I always wanted to be in the NHL, but after seeing him, I was craving it. When you are around long enough, it's pretty easy to separate the contenders from the pretenders, especially as it pertains to star players. Mario? He was no pretender. We all knew right away. There was no second guessing. We'd never seen the likes of him.

By this point, I'm getting a little frustrated. Let's put it this way: I knew the drive to Baltimore really well at this point. I was on a first-name basis with people in Breezewood, for Christ's sake.

The first couple of years, I knew I wasn't ready. Plus, the team had every reason to believe that I had some maturity issues. I had been arrested twice. I was still a young hockey player. But by 1985, I was getting a little annoyed, to be honest. I had this belief in myself and I was able to analyze myself pretty thoroughly. And you know what? I was getting pretty fucking good. Then I looked up at some of the guys at the NHL level. Greg Fox. Ville Siren. Kevin Maxwell. Even Rod Buskas. I mean, I'm not saying I was an elite NHL player or some star. But are you trying to tell me I wasn't better than those guys? My feelings were getting a little hurt, truth be told.

We'd get reports of people being hurt on the big team and, I admit, I'd get some anxiety in my stomach whenever there was an injury. I didn't like seeing people get hurt, but I was so damn ready. Many a day in my apartment in Baltimore would see me sitting around, staring at my phone. I would get called up to Pittsburgh for a few games here and there, but I was never able to stick, and I was never really sure why.

Thankfully, a big break was coming my way.

Our new coach in Baltimore was a guy named Gene Ubriaco. He was a veteran of minor league hockey. He always encouraged me, always made me feel good about myself. I was his guy, and he was mine.

And in the 1986–87 season, Gene changed my career. We had a meeting. He said, "We're going to try to do something different with you. I'm going to try you at forward. I think it can get you to the NHL. Are you up for it?"

Was I up for it? I'd have played goalie if Gene asked me to. He just had that persuasive personality and, at this point, I not only trusted him but was also hell bent on making it to the National Hockey League. I also had a center named Lemieux, which didn't hurt.

Oh, it wasn't Mario. But his big brother, Alain, was signed by the Penguins that year and put up more than 100 points in the AHL. What a hockey player he was. He didn't have Mario's size, his skating, or his overall talent level. Obviously. But he had these great hands. Not Mario hands, but legitimately great hands. He was some kind of a hockey player, a really brilliant player, so artistic, so gifted at distributing the puck. I started scoring goals on his wing. I put up 15 goals in half a season playing with him. The transition to the left wing wasn't so bad at all, to be honest with you. It's a hell of a lot easier to transition from defense to forward than it is from forward to the blue line. You could take the greatest forwards in the world and put them on the blue line, and I bet most of them would be lost even after considerable training. It's a different game, playing defense. But playing forward? Hell, I could do it. I was really fast, I was fearless, I was naturally responsible defensively because I was a defenseman by nature, and I could finish well enough. I wasn't Mike Bossy, but I could score goals. Alain and I developed a special kind of chemistry from Day 1. In the back of my mind, too, I was thinking to myself that I was making myself more valuable to the big club because I was so versatile.

I got a pretty long look with the big team in the 1987–88 season. Playing on defense, I put up 16 points in 21 games. I was finally feeling it, feeling like I belonged. We had a pretty good team and I was fitting in. We had just gotten a nice win in Los Angeles and, on February 15, 1988, we were practicing in Vancouver. That's when Pierre Creamer, the coach at the time, called me into his office.

"We're going to send you back down," Creamer said.

I responded, "Are you fucking kidding me? You've got to be kidding. Are you fucking kidding me?"

He said, "No, no. No. We're just going to go with a more veteran lineup. I want you to work on your game."

I said, "You're going to fucking regret this."

And I bet he did. When he decided to send me down, we had won five of our previous six games. We were a young team that was on a roll, starting to make some noise. Starting the next game in Vancouver, the Penguins lost five straight games while I was back in the American Hockey League. I'm not saying I'm the reason they lost five straight, but it goes to show Pierre made some bad decisions and that some serious mismanagement was taking place with those particular teams.

If you need any further proof, just consider how the Penguins' season ended.

It was a famous moment in Penguins history, in fact. They were playing in Washington on April 2, 1988. The Penguins were a legitimately good team at this point but were struggling to make the playoffs for the first time because the fucking Patrick Division was Murderer's Row. The Flyers were so good then. The Capitals were getting good. The Islanders weren't a dynasty anymore but still a playoff team. The Rangers were getting good. Even the Devils weren't that bad anymore and always gave us fits. And they all played so nasty.

Still, the Penguins had a chance to make the playoffs, but only if they won their last two games. That's what the math said. It was really a very simple concept. They needed four points in their last two games.

So, April 2 in Washington, the game was tied at 6–6 going to overtime. Mario had a hat trick in the first period, which says something about his talent and about his character. He was willing them at that point. All the goals were a thing of beauty that night.

On the bench, right before overtime, Pierre starts yelling at the guys, "Play for the tie! Play for the tie!" I wasn't there, but I've talked with guys about it. It's one of the most famous moments in franchise history and goes to show that Pierre was, shall we say, a little out of touch.

As fate would have it, of course, Mario took the puck with a minute left, blew past former teammate Larry Murphy and scored one of the iconic goals of his career, chipping the puck over Clint Malarchuk while crashing to the ice. It was one of those moments when he literally made something like that happen just because he could. Eddie Johnston, as the story goes, jumped up in the press box and yelled, "He's the best fucking player in the world." And he was. Was he ever. But he was surrounded by far too many people who just weren't competent.

The Penguins won their next game but still didn't make the playoffs. I think the Penguins hired a French guy to keep Mario happy, but let me tell you something, Mario didn't give a shit if you were French, English, European, American, whatever. He really didn't. He didn't look at those things. He wasn't that kind of a person. Mario just wanted to win and wanted to be surrounded by the people who could help him win. The Penguins were showing their ignorance if they thought having a French guy as his coach was what he needed.

To their credit, they quickly dismissed Pierre as their head coach following the season. And just like that, things were about to change for me.

In 1988, I was still working construction in the summer. I'm sure that sounds wild, but I wasn't making that much money in the AHL. It was enough to get by, enough to live comfortably, so I was still working some odd jobs in the summer. That summer, I was building medical offices for doctors. We had one phone on the whole site, which was actually nailed to a telephone pole. It essentially existed in the event of an emergency and for no other reason.

I've literally got plywood on top of my head when I get a call. "Hey Phil, there's a call for you."

I was terrified. The only person who had that number was my mom, and she'd never bother me with anything trivial while I was at work. I figured there was something seriously wrong. I run over to the phone. And the voice was a familiar one. It was Gene Ubriaco.

He was the new coach of the Pittsburgh Penguins, and he had a message for me.

"Bourquey," he said. "I was just hired as coach of the Pittsburgh Penguins. I just wanted you to know that you're my very first phone call. I just called your mom, and she gave me this number. Just so you know, you're on the team. I'll see you at training camp. Oh, and don't fuck it up. Don't embarrass me. I'll see you at camp."

I didn't even know what to think at that moment, but I've received a few breaks in my life, and I didn't want to miss out on taking advantage of this one. I was already in good shape, but I made sure I was in even better shape. I wanted to be at my best. He was so loyal to me and I didn't want to let him down.

I showed up at camp in September 1988 and I immediately felt at home. I was also quite excited about the talent we had assembled. Mario was on top of the world and was about to produce a 199-point season. He was only 23 then but he was, like EJ said, the best fucking player in the world. Something else had happened, too. The season before, the Penguins traded for Paul Coffey. It was one of the best moves in franchise history. Coff was an all-time great and he was also an incredibly good leader, a thoughtful guy who always said the right thing at the right time. We don't win Cups without him. He was that important in our transition from a shit team to a championship team.

Then there were the young, talented guys. Johnny Cullen. Mark Recchi. Kevin Stevens. Not only were they great players, but they were great characters. Every damn one of them.

Rex would go on to become one of my very best friends to this day. We lived together for a while and we just hit it off from Day 1. He had more talent than me—he's a Hall of Famer—but we had some things in common. We both had this chip on our shoulders. Mine was because I wasn't drafted, because I never seemed to be getting chances that I deserved. Rex was different. He had this chip on his shoulder because he was shorter than most players, and, as a result, talent evaluators didn't always take him seriously. What a big mistake.

I played on a line with Rex and Cullen a lot. I kind of got moved around. One game, I even got to play on Mario's line, and what a thrill that was. I was determined to stick in the NHL, and that was the year that it finally happened. I put up 17 goals and 43 points while playing all 80 games. I killed penalties. When they needed me to play on the blue line, I did it. Some guys would get insulted by that, but not me. I appreciated it. It made me feel wanted. It made me feel needed. I had a skill set that was unique and Gene knew that better than anyone.

Everything was coming together for me and I felt like that team was one big family. It would be like that for the rest of my days in Pittsburgh.

All of which brings us to the great Robbie Brown. Oh man. What a legend that guy was. He's one of my closest friends in hockey to this very day, in fact. This was the season that Robbie put up 49 goals while playing on Mario's right wing. Robbie couldn't skate for shit. I mean, he was so slow, a little out of shape, not very big. He didn't look the part. I guess he was an '80s version of Phil Kessel in some ways, but at least Phil can fly.

But Robbie and Mario made it work. They thought about the game the same way. Robbie could really finish, had great hands and incredible vision. He would go to these spots and Mario would know exactly what he was doing, and he would score every time. Bob Errey played on their left wing, and he was perfect there. He would do the dirty work, play defense, create turnovers, and those two would work their magic. It was something to see them go to work.

Robbie is one of the most talented, bizarre personalities I've ever played with, though. It's not a secret that he was dating Alyssa Milano at the time. Robbie was young. Alyssa was younger. But they had this sweet romance. And Robbie may have been the most loosey-goosey guy in the world. It was the same thing every damn game.

During intermissions, Robbie would take his sweater off and remove all his pads. He was just sitting there topless. It was his thing during those 15 minutes. Why? I have no idea. And there was always a phone in the trainer's room. So, right in front of all of us, he would very casually walk over to the phone. Alyssa was living in Los Angeles at that time.

He'd call her and say, "Hey babe, what's up? Well, we're doing well. We're winning 5–3. I've got a goal and two assists. Mario set me up for a real pretty back door play. So yeah, we're doing pretty well, just gotta hold on here in the third period. Well babe, I've got to go. Just wanted to call and tell you I love you. I'll talk with you tomorrow."

We thought it was hilarious. We were a bunch of young guns. Living the life, living the dream.

Things got a little awkward in December 1988, though. Robbie and Alyssa were dating and totally in love. December 19 was her 16th birthday party and she was actually in town with her family. Robbie gives me a call.

"Hey Bourquey, would you and your girlfriend mind coming to Christopher's on Mt. Washington? It's Alyssa's birthday party. Her dad and her brother are going to be there. I'm a little bit nervous. I don't want to be there alone, so I'm hoping you guys wouldn't mind coming."

I didn't mind, of course. But it was a little awkward. Here's this girl who is world famous at the time on *Who's the Boss?* and she's standing there in Christopher's, celebrating her Sweet 16 with her boyfriend, Robbie Brown.

She didn't come to Pittsburgh very often because she was so busy working in L.A. But she did come to games on occasion and we always visited with her when we'd have road trips in California. Things eventually didn't work out for Robbie and Alyssa. Imagine that, an actress and a hockey player couldn't work it out.

But I have to say, those were always fun times and we never really gave Robbie a hard time about it. He really loved her and was a good guy. The fact is, many of us were having the seasons of our lives and we were loving every minute of it. Every damn minute. We were the highest-scoring team in hockey on the ice, and I'd estimate we were doing pretty well off the ice, as well. We were on a roll, finally about to make the playoffs for the first time since 1982, Mario's first postseason run.

Before we got to that point, though, a little bit of unfinished business remained. Yeah, we could score everywhere. But not in Philadelphia.

We had gone 0–39–3 in our last 42 games in that city over a 15-year span. It was The Streak. And it was a real problem.

CHAPTER 5
PHILADELPHIA FREEDOM

It's hard for me to put into words how good we were getting and, in particular, how great Mario was during the 1988–89 season. He put up 199 points, only 16 shy of Wayne Gretzky's all-time record. But let's keep some other things in mind here. He missed four games with an injury. While Robbie and Bobby were good linemates for him, they weren't exactly Jari Kurri or Glenn Anderson. And did I mention the Patrick Division?

We did our bet to protect Mario every single night, make no mistake. We had a lot of tough guys, Jay Caufield chief among them. And guys like me were always willing to drop the gloves on his behalf. Always. But there was only so much we could do to protect Mario. He took an ungodly beating every night in divisional games. On October 30, 1988, a Rangers defenseman named David Shaw whacked Mario in the throat in a really scary incident at MSG. Mario was really hurt. We went nuts. Dan Quinn, one of Mario's best friends at the time, went after Shaw and speared him. A huge melee ensued. We decided to not let Shaw off the ice when he was kicked out of the game. We walked over to where the Rangers left the ice to head toward the locker room and formed a wall so he couldn't leave the ice. We all wanted to beat the shit out of him, and that was the plan. The NYPD had other ideas and made us take a step back so that he could escape.

When we saw the Rangers a few weeks later, on the annual Thanksgiving Eve game, Mario drilled them with three big hits on his first shift. The Igloo went wild. He ended up putting up a goal and five assists in that game as he exacted some personal revenge. It was beautiful. But it was also taxing for him to deal with this kind of stuff on a regular basis. Mario was a big guy, so he was never protected by referees the way Gretzky was. If you played the game then, trust me, you knew what the rules were. Gretzky was never to be touched. But it was open season on Mario. I don't know if it's because he was so big, or because he was French, or if it's because he wasn't Gretzky. I don't know, and I've never known, but it always made us angry. Mario was a big man and could take care of himself, but it's not like we wanted the greatest hockey player in the world fighting. Absolutely nobody wanted anything to do with that. And the better he played, the more ferocious the beatings became. I really started to notice it during this season.

It's difficult to put Mario's greatness that season into perspective. He came out in another galaxy in October of the 1988–89 season, producing 42 points in his first 12 games. Yeah. He was that good.

We'd sit on the bench and look at each other. And we'd literally start laughing. We didn't know what else to do. Every time you thought you saw the most incredible play, he'd do something else. You think you've seen it all in the NHL. You should be difficult to really impress. But he did it every single night. The show absolutely never stopped.

But the better he played, the more the abuse intensified. It still makes me angry when I think about it. And while the Rangers were especially dirty back then, and all the Patrick Division teams possessed a vicious streak, there was one team that was a little different. You'll never guess who it was.

The Flyers earned their reputation for being the nastiest team in the league. It's how they built their teams year in and year out. Sure, they wanted talent, they wanted to be good, they wanted to win. But above all else, they wanted to intimidate. And you know what? They pulled it off quite nicely. They were big, bad, and nasty. They wanted to fight and were perfectly happy to pull some dirty tricks in Pittsburgh. But in Philly, things were completely different. Everything about The Spectrum was designed to intimidate. The fans were rowdy, vulgar, and always talked a big game. There was just a darkness about the place. The Flyers wanted us to be a little wary when we walked into that place, and I promise you we were.

The Streak went on for 15 years. Imagine that. Back then, you played divisional teams seven times in a season, so sometimes you'd play four times per season in a given building. And the Pittsburgh Penguins had gone 15 years without winning there. My God.

Then, along came February 2, 1989.

It had gotten pretty ridiculous by this point. At the same time, we were so confident. We knew it was going to happen soon. They could intimidate all they wanted, but eventually the bullshit stops and the team with all the talent in the world is going to win. No one in Pittsburgh thought it was possible, as I recall. The day of the game in Philly was unreal.

Scott Paulsen and Jimmy Krenn, who were in charge of the WDVE morning show at the time, showed up in Philly on the day of the game. Before the game, they're doing witch doctor shit at the arena. It was such a circus. Scott and Jimmy had to catch a flight home immediately after their stunt, so they didn't get to see the game, which is a shame. Or perhaps it's better that they got the hell out of Dodge when they did.

Hell, I remember being on 3WS Radio before the game. They had Robbie and me on as special guests. And you know what they did? They brought in a hypnotist. Really. They tried to hypnotize us into playing well in Philly for a change. That's how big of a deal the streak was in Pittsburgh three decades ago. Not only had we not won there in 15 years, but it was never even close. It was a profound embarrassment on most nights.

We started Wendell Young in net that night. Make that former Flyers farmhand Wendell Young. That night, he was unreal. The Flyers bombarded him with shots and had breakaways and great looks most of the game. And Wendell denied them time and time again. He stopped 39 of 42 shots that night, and those shots weren't floaters from the point.

We went up 1–0 in the first period when Johnny Cullen scored on the power play. He was becoming such a good player, and it's frustrating to me that people always forget how good he was.

Later in the first, Johnny set me up and I beat Ron Hextall for my 15th goal of the season. The game went back and forth, but by the end of the second period, we had taken a 4–1 lead. In the third period, we had to hang on for dear life, of course. They pulled within 4–2, but then Danny Quinn scored and that gave us the breathing room we needed. We held on to win it 5–3. They tried some of their typical Flyers antics as things got nasty in the third period. Dicky Tocchet beat the shit out of Jimmy Johnson. They made one final push. But we weren't having any of it. Slowly but surely, we were maturing and become a great hockey team. They could try and bully us all they wanted, but it wasn't going to work that night. Even without Mario scoring a goal, we won in Philly. How about that? Granted, he played an amazing game that night, setting up two goals and totally shutting them down defensively every time he was on the still. Yet, the fact that he didn't score and yet we still won that night provided plenty of evidence that we were maturing. We hadn't arrived just yet. But we were on our way, and moments like this were undeniably important.

What a scene it was in the locker room after the game. I'm not embarrassed to admit that we celebrated like it was Game 7 of the Stanley Cup Final. It was that big of a deal to us and it was the best moment of my career at that point. You have to understand what it was like in that building. My God, their fans were so awful. Really ruthless people. Yeah, they were great fans and they cared about their hockey team very much. That's great. But those people really crossed the line personally on a regular basis.

They threw stuff at you. They knew things about your personal life. There were no boundaries. And it wasn't just players. Our media was treated like shit there. Our trainers, doctors, equipment staff. You name it. They were all treated like dirt in that building. While it was just a regular season victory on paper, it was so, so much more to us. I'll never forget it. The Flyers, you must understand, were an extension of their fans. They didn't just want to beat you on the scoreboard; they really did want to beat the shit out of you. It was their obsession. They literally wanted to beat you up and send you to the hospital, and quite often, that's precisely what happened. Paul Holmgren. Dave Brown. Craig Berube. I could go on and on with the names. Even their great players, like Tim Kerr, Tocchet, and Rod Brind'Amour, were tough bastards who were always willing to pummel you. You know how you never saw Tocchet lose a fight? There's a reason for that. He wasn't the biggest guy in the world, but no one ever fucked with him because, pound for pound, he may have been the league's toughest man. They just lived for the beatings that they gave teams. They really did. If they were up 8–1 with two minutes left, they'd send the knuckleheads out to beat the shit out of us one last time, just to send a message for the next time we'd meet. They always wanted to add that exclamation point. They were obsessed with it, I think. The "Philly Flu" was a real thing. People would take the morning skate there and suddenly came down with an illness and were unable to play. Go figure. It's funny how often that seemed to happen against those guys in that city.

You know, everything changed for us on that night, when we finally beat them. It was a massive hurdle for us. Mario had never won a game there and had taken so many beatings there. I remember how happy he was after that game. It was a big deal psychologically. Also, I think there was legitimately some pride in the fact that we were doing things the proper way. Sure, we had some tough customers. It was the '80s. Everybody had tough customers and we were no different. You needed them. We were not, however, promoting that kind of shit. We really weren't. We were promoting fast, exciting hockey. We were about scoring goals. We were about the beautiful game. We were about Mario. Other teams in the league, especially the Flyers, weren't so interested in those kinds of things. But we were different, and I think a lot of it was because of Mario. He wanted us to play a certain way, to be an entertaining team. He was a showman on the ice if ever there's been one, and we emulated that a little bit. Sure, gooning it up can be entertaining. People enjoy seeing fights in games every now and then, no doubt. But not that many people were going to games because of the violent element. They wanted to be entertained, to witness true greatness. We had that in Mario and we followed his lead that season. Things were starting to happen for us. It was a special time.

And yeah, winning in Philly was a step. The thinking was, *If we can win here, we can absolutely win anywhere. Oh, hell yes we can.* We started to become the Penguinees then. It was a mindset, a confidence. It didn't matter how many goals we were down on a given night. It really didn't matter. We knew we had more talent than other teams and we had this incredible belief. Years later, we would become known for pulling off incredible postseason comebacks, and I think it all started during the 1988–89 season. So much of it goes back to that night in Philadelphia. What a damn night.

We clinched a playoff spot for the first time since 1982. What a big deal. For guys like Mario, Bobby, Troy Loney, and me, it was an especially big thing. During this time, a lot of us gravitated toward The Doctor, Paul Coffey. See, Coff was the only guy on that team with a ring. And he had three of them. He knew what it took. He had already taken that journey with the Oilers. He had a special kind of attitude about him, a special leadership quality. He would literally look at us and say, "Listen, just follow me, boys." That was him. That was Coff. He wasn't just a Hall of Fame player, but he taught us how to be professionals. In many ways, bringing him to Pittsburgh was the greatest trade in Penguins history. He really did show the way.

We got the Rangers in the first round of the playoffs, which was a good thing. We just enjoyed playing against them. They were good, but we had a gear they didn't have. Plus, Phil Esposito had just fired their coach and was behind the bench himself. Things were a real mess in New York during that stretch. Meanwhile, our general manager at the time, Tony Esposito, was pushing a lot of the right buttons. We felt good going into that series and definitely felt like we were the favorites. Apparently, we were. We swept the Rangers in four games. Mario played defense like we'd never seen him play during that series. The truly great players always know to elevate their games on the biggest stages. That was Mario in the 1989 playoffs.

I have to say, we probably felt a little satisfied following that series. We had never won a damn thing before, so to get through to the second round of the playoffs was such a huge deal for us. I wouldn't say we were totally satisfied, but I suppose our immaturity was probably somewhat on display. In retrospect, we probably weren't quite ready to make a team run because emotionally we just weren't there yet. Still, we were on a roll and feeling good about ourselves in the second round. And the Flyers were waiting after upsetting the Capitals in the opening around.

We split the first two games of the series. Game 3 was a Friday night in Philly. I was in the starting lineup, and when I went to the red line for the opening draw, Berube skated up to me. "When the puck drops, we're going," he said.

Christ. I knew how that was going to go. But what was I going to do, turtle? Hell no, I wasn't. That wouldn't be a very good look.

We wanted to prove that we were no longer intimidated by playing in the Spectrum, so the last thing I was going to do was back down from that kind of a challenge. He beat the shit out of me, of course. He had me throttled throughout the fight, bent over. But you know what? I showed up and I took that beating, and I kept playing. That meant a lot to my teammates. We weren't going to be intimidated.

I had a good game and was playing some with Mario and Robbie. The game went to overtime. Then came one of the greatest moments of my life.

Robbie came skating down the left wing and hit me with a perfect backdoor pass. I buried it past Hextall to give us the overtime victory. At that point, it was without question the greatest moment of my career. I celebrated like a wild man. Never in my wildest dreams did I think I'd score a goal like that on the biggest stage like that. In overtime? Playoffs? In Philly? Get the hell out of here. But it happened. It really did happen, and it was an amazing time.

We probably started feeling a little too good about ourselves at this point. But again, we were kids. The series went back and forth. We got our assess kicked in Game 4. Mario hurt his neck in that game and there was concern he wouldn't be able to play in Game 5.

So, did he play in Game 5? Well, he had a hat trick six minutes into the game. Scored four goals in the first period. Finished with five goals and three assists. So yeah, he played. It was one of the greatest performances in NHL history. And he was hurt, playing against a team that was trying to hurt him even more. Think about that.

But we started playing like shit in the third period. We "held on" to win 10–7 and they used that momentum to beat us convincingly in Game 6. So it was back to the Igloo for the decisive Game 7, the winner getting a trip to Montreal for the Wales Conference Final. Boy, that would have meant a lot to Mario, who was Montreal's favorite son.

We lost 4–1. Our future goalie, Kenny Wregget, got the start and kicked our ass. He was awesome that game. We didn't play badly at all. Trust me, we didn't. We were pretty good that night, but Kenny was just too much. He was one of those goalies who could get really streaky. And he was streaky that night in a good way for the Flyers. That one stung a lot. But I suppose it's good to lose a series like that for a hockey team. The greatest teams of all time all had that series that was a punch to the gut. It can make a young team stronger, no question about it. It really does fuel you, because you don't ever want to feel that sting again. Plus, I think that series taught us some lessons about overconfidence. It's okay to be confident. But it's not okay to be overconfident.

We actually stayed at the William Penn Hotel in Pittsburgh the night before Game 7. It was pretty common for teams to stay at hotels even at home during the playoffs back then. We ate together before Game 7 and we had our bags packed for Montreal. If we won, we were flying straight there that night. I still remember walking from the hotel to the Civic Arena before Game 7. What an awkward feeling that was. Talk about tempting fate. I think there was bad karma in the air that night. We didn't really know any better. We didn't know what the hell we were doing. But a part of us, I believe, was thinking about making that trip to Montreal instead of focusing on the task at hand. You live, you learn.

And let me tell you, we learned a hell of a lot during that season. We learned we could beat anyone at any time. We finally won in Philly. We swept a good Rangers team. We knew we were better than the Flyers and should have beaten them. We should have been in the conference finals. And we were still so damn young. We were young. We were hungry. And we were on our way.

We knew Mario was, by far at that point, the world's greatest hockey player and that nothing was going to change any time soon.

We knew we were playing in a real hockey town at that point. When you think of Pittsburgh, you think of the Steelers. But they weren't any good in the 1980s. The Pirates were getting really good with a young guy named Barry Bonds in left field. But Pittsburgh was becoming a hockey town. The crowds in that postseason at the Igloo were absolutely off the charts. People were into us. They liked how we played, they liked our personalities. It was special to be a part of it every day.

On a personal level, I was learning that I was a damn good NHL player. If they needed me to go play defense, I'd take that tap on the shoulder and do it. I played on the point with Coffey on the power play at various points during the season. But I was a left wing and a good one. I was scoring 20 goals at the NHL level and was a dependable penalty killer. There are only so many players who can provide that kind of thing, and I was well aware of it. I finally belonged, and I had a head coach who truly believed in me. That's a very big combination for a young hockey player.

So yeah, when I think of the 1988–89 season, all I can do is smile. We didn't win anything that year, not even a division title. But we did win a playoff series, and, at that point, we were on our way. I was on my way. There was an energy associated with that team that was just a little different. Coming to the rink every day was truly an honor because you knew something special could happen at any time.

We still had our lessons to learn and still had some beatings to take. We didn't know what kind of adversity would be ahead, and, in hockey, you realize that there is always going to be adversity. But that season was special and will always have a special place in my heart. The greatest player of all time was absolutely putting on a show, and we weren't just along for the ride. We were complementing him. We were along for the ride with him. All of Pittsburgh was along for the ride.

The fun—and the hard times—were just beginning.

CHAPTER 6

THE LOST SEASON

Everything in life was pretty good in the summer of 1989. I was finally an NHL regular, making more than $100,000 a year—back then, that was pretty good money in the world of professional sports—and playing for a team that was about to become something special. It was so awesome.

Personally, everything was great. I was totally comfortable playing on the left wing, I was comfortable with the Penguins and, in Pittsburgh, there was no question I had found my home. Plus, my favorite coach was behind the bench. Perfect.

But the 1989–90 season wasn't so perfect. In fact, it was miserable. From October on, anything that could have gone wrong did. Were we getting a little full of ourselves? I suppose that's a possibility. There was probably an element of that, yes. But we also had horrible adversity to deal with.

Mario's back was an absolute mess. He had been fairly healthy in his first five NHL seasons, only missing some games because of minor injuries. Starting in the fall of 1989, though, Mario's back became a big problem, and it would remain that way for the rest of his career.

So, Mario's back was a mess, and while he was still Mario, he wasn't dominating like he had the previous season. He was looking to pass more frequently, looking for the trailer a lot after he would enter the zone, stuff like that. Mario was the best one-on-one player of all time, but he wasn't looking to beat guys as often. That's how you knew he didn't feel right. Then consider that his relationship with Gene Ubriaco wasn't so good. Paul Coffey didn't like Ubi, either. I was right in the middle of it all. He was my favorite coach. Hell, my teammates liked to say that my dad was coaching me from behind the bench. It was pretty much true. But at the same time, I adore Mario. And Coffey is one of my favorite teammates ever. So, there was an awful lot of drama swirling around our team at that time because of the strained relationship between Ubi and Mario. It was becoming a bigger and bigger deal.

Ubi, meanwhile, was becoming a marked man in Pittsburgh. Listen, I always loved the guy. He was my guy and he always will be. But he did have a certain swagger about him and, in Pittsburgh, if you have that kind of swagger, you're not always going to be popular. Ubi did himself no favors by how he handled things that season. During that time, coaches would have to walk around the glass at Civic Arena to get to and from the bench. Ubi didn't like that route because it meant the fans could mock him while he walking around the glass. So, instead, Ubi found a way to crawl from the locker room under the seats and to the bench. I love the guy, but that wasn't a great look. I don't really know why the fans were so hard on him, but they were. It was more of a blue-collar crowd back then, not the polite crowd you see today at PPG Paints Arena. They let him hear it all the time.

That wasn't the only adversity. Tommy Barrasso's daughter, Ashley, was diagnosed with cancer during that season and wasn't given a favorable prognosis. Tommy had to leave the team for a while during her treatments. What a strange time for the team. Tommy was understandably very sensitive about the situation. We didn't ask many questions. He was sensitive to begin with and we didn't want to upset him more by asking invasive questions about her.

So that's where we stood. There were so many good players on that team and young guys like Kevin Stevens, John Cullen, and Mark Recchi were starting to make a real impact. But the obstacles were huge. Still, I was thriving on a personal level. I scored a career-high 22 goals that season, and my entire game was evolving nicely. I was an effective two-way winger and actually got some time on Mario's line that season. Playing on his line was always such an honor. No one was worthy of being on that line, and we all knew it.

During this time, my confidence level as a player was rising. I was seeing some time on Mario's line and, when I wasn't with him, I was still surrounded by talented guys. I was trusted by the coaching staff and I was thriving. I was also seeing some time on the top power play. As a defenseman by trade, I had been playing the point on the power play my entire life. I could still pull it off pretty well. The quarterback of that power play, of course, was Coffey. Mike Lange called him "The Doctor" for a reason. He was always in charge and he was maybe the greatest defenseman ever at skating the puck through the neutral zone in order to set up the power play. He had a cannon of a shot and incredible vision. Yeah, he was that guy. Mario would set up shop in the left wing circle. Really, as long as you had those two guys working the power play, you couldn't go wrong. If you were putting together a list of the five greatest power play guys ever to play on a power play, Mario and Coffey would make that list. Easily. But still, three other guys have to be effective out there with them, and I saw some time on the point that season. On the surface, it sounds intimidating. When you're surrounded by greatness, you don't want to fail. But I can honestly say it wasn't intimidating at all. Mario wanted the puck but he didn't make you feel uncomfortable in the least. He had a subtle way of telling you what to do. If he wanted the puck, he'd let out a little noise, and you knew to give him the puck. It was pretty simple, honestly. And Coffey was just so great. Truly one of the greatest teammates I've ever had. He had a simple way of relating to everyone on a hockey team. He knew that, other than Mario, he had more talent than anyone on our roster. But it's not like we viewed him as "Paul Coffey, superstar defenseman who we somehow got from the Edmonton Oilers." Nah, it wasn't ever like that, not from his very first day in Pittsburgh, because he's just not that kind of person. He's truly one of the greatest teammates I've ever had, and he had a humble nature about him. Coff was a superstar, a future Hall of Famer who had scored 48 goals in one season (let that sink in for a moment). He was intelligent, wealthy, good-looking, and had charisma for days. Not a bad combination, huh? But he was just such a pro, such a legitimately good guy. One time, when Coffey was still pretty new to the Penguins, I was still slightly in awe of him. Coff's a smart guy, so I'm sure he recognized this. He was this future Hall of Famer and I was just this young kid from Boston trying to stick in the NHL. I was sitting there after practice minding my own business when he approached me. "Hey Bourquey," he said. "Let's go have lunch." That was Paul Coffey. He never considered himself to be bigger than the team in any way. He learned so much playing in Edmonton. There were a lot of great leaders on those Oilers teams. Yeah, they had talent, but they also had a perfect blend of personalities. Coffey was one of those guys for sure, and he took what he learned there and made us a better locker room from the very beginning.

Ubriaco and our general manager, Tony Esposito, were fired in the middle of the season. It put me in a hell of a spot. We had so much success the year before, but the 1989–90 Penguins were struggling, and, quite honestly, Mario didn't like Ubi. Neither did Coff. They were our two leaders, and they just couldn't stand the guy. It got pretty ugly. When Ubi was fired, he said, "Coaching Mario Lemieux is like trying to teach a shark table manners." I think that quote haunted Gene for the rest of his life because Mario was no coach killer. Coff came out and ripped Ubi afterward, basically calling him a minor league coach. Ubi accused Mario and Coff of "deserting him" during the final two weeks of his tenure. Those are pretty powerful words about two of the greatest hockey players of all time. It was just a personality thing with Mario and Ubi. Mario is a quiet, humble man. But he's also extremely prideful. I loved how Ubi dealt with me, but a lot of guys didn't care for his brashness, and I definitely think that was part of the problem. Ubi was replaced by a guy named Craig Patrick. Truth be told, I knew absolutely nothing about Craig. This whole situation, incidentally, led to one of the more embarrassing moments of my career.

In our first game with Craig behind the bench, I scored two goals. To be honest, my scoring two goals was pretty much a "fuck you" to the Penguins. Gene was my guy, the guy who gave me my chance. I wasn't feeling very secure at that point in time. The one guy who always had my back was gone for good, and I felt pretty alone. But I had to go out there and prove myself, so that's exactly what I did. But I had a defiant streak back then, and it was on display after the game that night. The media wanted to speak with me because I had a good game and because the reporters knew I had a close relationship with Ubi. They wanted to get my take. And I knew it. There wasn't that much media coverage of the Penguins back then, maybe four or five people. I went to hide in the trainer's room. A member of the media relations staff came to get me. I refused to talk. I told him I'd come out, but then I stayed. Finally, after about the fifth time he requested me, I came out to chat. It was probably one of the most arrogant moments of my life. I was just so damn bitter at that point in time. I knew the media hates it when you make them wait like that. It comes across as a dick move, and quite honestly, that's exactly what it was. But I was just steaming angry at that point in time.

The funny thing is, Ubi was a good coach. He had great success in the IHL for many, many more years after his run in Pittsburgh. But he was never offered another NHL coaching job. Ever.

We started to play better under Craig, who was also hired to be our general manager. He was a genius. At the time, he was known for being Herb Brooks' quiet, intelligent assistant coach on the 1980 U.S. Olympic Team. As it would turn out, the guy was a genius general manager and talent evaluator. He wasn't a bad coach, either. He was incredibly quiet and relied on his assistants a great deal. But he was so damn smart. You could just sense it. And he was one of those guys who would really make you feel good when he complimented you, because he didn't dish out compliments very often. You know what he was doing then? He was studying us. That's absolutely what he was doing. He realized there was Stanley Cup talent on that team. Hell, everyone realized that. But Craig knew he had to orchestrate a plan to get us over the top. I think he knew the 1989–90 Penguins weren't going anywhere, but his work had already begun.

Here's the thing, though. The Penguins of that era, as damn talented and special as we were, still needed Mario. He was the best player in the world. He was in so much pain, though. And it kept getting worse. Somehow, he started to play better as the pain intensified. How that's possible, I will never know. But it started to happen that season.

Mario started building a scoring streak during the season. When it got to 10 games, it was no big deal. He always did that. Twenty was impressive. But it kept soaring. Gretzky had the all-time record at 51, a number believed to be untouchable. Mario just kept scoring and kept ignoring the pain. I'll never forget snapshots from that season.

By January, Mario was never practicing. I mean, never. It hurt too much to practice. While the rest of us were practicing, he was getting treatment on his back. While the rest of us were at morning skates, Mario was getting more treatment. Everything that was done was done to get Mario on the ice for games. He was only 24 and, looking back at it, he probably should have stopped playing that season and gotten the proper medical attention so that the rest of his career wouldn't be in jeopardy. This guy was an unreal competitor though. No one talks about that with Mario. They talk about the incomparable talent and, yes, it was. No one seems to be interested in talking about what a warrior he was on the ice, how he would will us to victory and how he would ignore pain to put on a nightly show. That's what he did during this particular season.

It was the same old routine, really. When you're in the locker room before a game, there's a clock in there. With two minutes remaining before the start of a game or a period, someone always yells, "Two minutes!" We'd look around, and Mario would never be at his locker. We'd see his gloves and shoulder pads sitting there, but no Mario. Then someone would yell, "One minute!" At that point, we'd always go take the ice, not knowing if he was joining us or not. That's the level of pain he was in and that's the level of uncertainty that we always felt. Invariably, right before the start of a period, there he would be, walking onto the ice. His treatments were set up so that he always had enough time to make it back before the start of a period. Sometimes, he'd miss part of a period if the adjustment didn't go well or if his medication made him sick. But he always came back out. It was always a special thing at home games at the Igloo. You could sense the restlessness in the crowd when Mario didn't appear at the start of a period. Then, you'd hear the crowd absolutely erupt when he returned to the ice. We had a lot of great players, but when you showed up to watch the Penguins play, you were only watching one guy at that time.

I truly don't believe people understand what he went through during those years, this one especially. It was unreal, painful to watch. On airplanes, he couldn't lift his bags into the overhead compartment. Imagine that. Here's this powerful, 6-foot-4 guy, and he couldn't lift his luggage. That's the level of pain he was always in.

At the time, a guy named Tracy Luppe handled our sticks for us. His job, among many others, was to get Mario's skates tied properly. He was in so much pain, especially during his scoring streak, that he couldn't tie his own skates. Can you imagine that? One of our team carpenters actually made a device to help Mario out. It was basically a wooden stool, kind of like the things you see at shoe stores. It was designed to help Mario get his skate on so he wouldn't have to bend all the way over. Some nights, most nights, really, he just couldn't do it. So Tracy would be there to get his skates tied. I can still hear Mario in my mind saying things like, "That's a little too tight" or, "A little tighter, please." Mario was so great with all the people in the organization. I've never seen him big-time anyone, not one time. All these people were working to get his body, bad back and all, on the ice. If you see old clips of him from that season, you'll see that Mario couldn't get on the ice traditionally by hopping over the boards. He would always sit where the door opened on the bench to make it easier. Or, if he couldn't sit there, he would pull his legs over the boards so that he didn't have to bend over or show any flexibility. It was ridiculous, the whole thing. He shouldn't have been playing, but nobody was going to tell Mario Lemieux what to do. And the thing is, after a slow start to the season, he started to play extremely well. I've never seen a damn thing like it. The streak made it to 30 games. And then 40 games. We didn't really talk about it on the bench. We'd just say things to him like, "Keep it going, big guy." Stuff like that. It's like when a pitcher has a no-hitter, you just prefer to avoid him.

He felt better on some days than others. The NHL All-Star Game was in Pittsburgh and, back then, that game was a much bigger deal. Pittsburgh was still trying to make it as a hockey town and Mario knew it was important that he played. So he went out and scored four goals, including a hat trick in the first period. Always the showman.

The show finally stopped on Valentine's Day in New York. Halfway through the second period, Mario left the game against the Rangers and didn't come back. The pain he was in that night was just too much. He barely missed extending his streak, setting up Johnny Cullen, only to see him hit the post. We actually won the game that night, but Mario had to leave. The pain was just intolerable. After the game, Craig said, "Mario needs medical attention now."

Mario went out to the West Coast for a while to have doctors take a look at his back. It wasn't pretty, and they recommended that he didn't play for the remainder of the season. When we had our West Coast swing, Mario was in the crowd watching the game. And he was sitting beside Tommy Barrasso because Ashley was in California getting her cancer treatments. What a sobering thing to see, our star and our goaltender in street clothes, battling something much bigger than the L.A. Kings.

We didn't talk about the situation with Tommy's daughter all that much. We didn't know how bad it was, not a clue. As it turned out, she had poor odds of living, something like 15 percent. Thankfully Ashley was a fighter and, to this day, she's a very healthy and successful young woman in Pittsburgh. It's a great ending to a tough story. And it makes you think of all the tragedy the Penguins have endured over the years. Players and executives have had fatal car accidents. There have been more cancer diagnoses then I care to remember. It goes on and on. It's part of the Penguins, all this tragedy and adversity. It would have destroyed lesser organizations, lesser groups of people. But it made us stronger in the long run. It made us the Penguins.

Mario's incredible scoring surge had put us back into playoff position after a bad start. Back then, four out of six Patrick Division teams made the playoffs. That doesn't sound like too difficult of a thing, but again, please remember that every team in that division was good during this time. It was incredible. Every shit team in the league was in a different division. If you played in any other division, four out of five teams got in, and one of those teams was always awful. So it wasn't an easy thing for us.

When Mario left the lineup, we stumbled. Tommy missed a lot of time, too. It was a little too much for us to handle. We didn't completely fall apart, but suddenly, making the playoffs became a difficult proposition. We did everything we could and still had plenty of good players. But Mario wasn't just the greatest player in the world...he was our heartbeat. We didn't really have that same belief without the big boy around.

As things worked out, we had to get a point against the Buffalo Sabres in our final game of the regular season to reach the postseason. Otherwise, the Islanders would get in. Talk about pressure. The game still meant something to the Sabres, by the way. With one point, they'd get home ice advantage in their first round series.

So, guess who shows up on the day of the game? Yep, there was No. 66 on his white horse, as only he could. What a man.

I'm no doctor, but I can tell you, without question, that Mario shouldn't have played that night. Whatever was wrong with his back was still wrong. He was still in pain, still struggling to be flexible in any way. But the thing people need to understand about Mario is what an incredibly prideful man he is. Missing the playoffs would have been an embarrassment in his mind, and he was our captain, our leader, our best player. He couldn't imagine missing that game if winning it could get us into the postseason. So he showed up. Remember, this was Mario; no one was going to tell him what to do.

He set up a goal early in the game and then scored in the second period, helping us even the game at 2–2. He hadn't played in six weeks and was in immense pain. He hadn't practiced. I don't even know if he skated during that time. I'd guess he probably didn't.

But there he was, putting up two points against a very hungry team. Only Mario.

It wasn't meant to be, though. The game went to overtime. We were five scoreless minutes away from getting into the tournament. Uwe Krupp took a harmless-looking shot from the point that bounced off a body and into the net. I couldn't fucking believe it. I felt totally empty inside. It was probably the biggest gut-punch loss of my life. We were all devastated.

You must understand that we didn't make as much money back then, but most of us had certain bonuses in our contract that were a pretty big deal. "Score 20 goals and make the playoffs, extra $20,000." Stuff like that. So, while losing the game was the biggest issue that night, I was also out a lot of money, and I wasn't alone.

After the game was over, a bunch of us decided to go drinking. It seemed like the reasonable course of action at the time. We went to a bar in Robinson Township. Mario couldn't come out because he was in so much pain he had to get even more treatment following the game.

But Coff was there, as were Johnny Cullen, Mark Recchi, Artie Stevens, and a few other guys. It's funny, but back then, salaries weren't public knowledge the way they are now. We didn't have the Internet and salary caps. Nobody really knew how much money everyone else was making and it's not something that was talked about. Guys respected the privacy involved with it. But we finally started to talk a little bit that night. We didn't talk about how much we were specifically making or anything like that. It wasn't that invasive. But I remember guys saying, "Well, that cost me $20,000. How about you? And how about you?" And we're just sitting there, drinking beer and talking about how much fucking money we had all lost, all because of fucking Uwe Krupp. Are you serious? A shot from the point like that? And how the hell did we lose after Mario just risked his career to come help us win?

Yeah, that was a low point for that group at that point in time. We knew we were good, we knew we had potential to be a Cup team. And I am a big believer that the all-time greats have to get that kick to the balls at some point. It makes you stronger. Makes you hate losing a little bit more. Commits you to seeing things all the way through, no matter what. I even remember thinking at the time that maybe a loss like this would serve us well down the road.

But sitting there getting drunk in Robinson, I didn't feel any better, to be quite honest. I had just finished the best season of my career statistically and I was finally established. Thank God for that. But I'd just lost out on a lot of money, my favorite coach was gone for good, and we really didn't know what the future held for Mario. His back condition was seriously scary shit.

Plus, we knew Craig wanted to be the general manager. He didn't really want to be the coach, so I had no idea who the new coach of the Penguins would be. Hell, I'd been in the organization for seven years and there had already been six head coaches. I finally had my guy who trusted me, and now I was going to have to prove myself all over again.

The incredible buzz that the 1988–89 season had produced was now in the rearview mirror. The 1989–90 season prompted us to question ourselves, and for good reason. I wasn't really sure what the future held for me, for Mario, or for the Pittsburgh Penguins. On the surface, none of this should have been so difficult. Look at the talent we had put together, for Christ's sake. It was hard, though. The Penguins weren't born to be winners. Remember, throughout their history, they hadn't won a damn thing. For some franchises, it comes effortlessly. Not for the Penguins. There was always bad karma, always bad luck, always some form of adversity waiting to kick us in the ass. And we knew it. You could sense it when you played for the Penguins in those days.

That summer was rough. Great hope remained because of the talent that we had, but there was also great uncertainty. More than anything, I could always sense this negative vibe, people always basically expecting the worst. What a shitty feeling, always thinking something is about to go bad. Now that I look back on it, we really needed someone who was a positive influence on us, someone who could ignore all the bad stuff and focus on the good. A glass-half-full kind of guy.

Yeah, that's what the Pittsburgh Penguins needed.

CHAPTER 7
BADGER BOB JOHNSON TO THE RESCUE

We were still struggling with how the 1989–90 season ended. We were good that year, Mario came back to save our season when he literally needed someone to tie his skate for him before the game, and we still couldn't make the playoffs. We were kind of reeling from that.

Then, we hired a new coach: Badger Bob Johnson.

No one realized at that time how much our lives were about to change. All we really knew about Bob was that he was a college coach and that he'd had some success with the Calgary Flames. That was it. We knew nothing about him, but I can tell you there was a stigma associated with guys who were primarily college coaches. A big stigma. Those kinds of guys aren't always taken very seriously. How many college coaches have made that jump from NCAA to the NHL? And how many have actually been good? Not that many, really, and we knew it. Don't get me wrong, we understood it. Craig was a USA Hockey guy. Bob was a USA Hockey guy. Bob had the reputation of being a good coach. So, it all made enough sense. But we weren't really sure what to make of it.

Things then got really weird. We received information in August that our training camp for the 1990–91 season would be held in Vail, Colorado. Seriously? What the fuck were the Pittsburgh Penguins doing in Vail, Colorado? We had some conversations with one another before that camp, and we all thought it was beyond strange.

Once we got to know Badger Bob, though, it all started to make sense.

Don't get me wrong, Vail is a great place. We weren't complaining, but we didn't really understand the thinking behind it. Then we started to realize some things. Bob was a bit of a tree hugger. This was a human being who had a real appreciation for nature, who loved being outdoors, and he always wanted to share that love with everyone. Plus, Bob had other things in mind. He knew we could score and that we could skate other teams off the rink. But to pull that off, you also have to be in tremendous condition. Training in a high altitude is something a lot of players do these days, but back then, it wasn't really a thing for hockey players. But Bob was way ahead of his time in that regard and wanted us training in the mountains. Looking back on it, that was a brilliant plan for our team.

It didn't take long for us to realize that Bob was different. He wasn't like any hockey coach or any human being I've ever known. We were at this rink in downtown Vail during one of our first practices. We were doing this horseshoe drill, which anyone who's ever played hockey knows is an easy passing drill.

The drill was open to the public, so there were some people in the building watching us skate. Right in the middle of this, Bob skated over to the scorer's desk and grabbed a live microphone. He then started giving play by play of the entire practice for everyone in attendance. It was unbelievable. He started telling the fans about each drill, describing what we were doing and how it would make us better hockey players. Then he would walk up to each player and basically introduce them to the crowd. I can still hear him saying in that raspy voice of his, "Up next is Kevin Stevens, everyone. He's a big, strapping left wing from Boston, Massachusetts. I want you all the keep an eye on this kid this season. I'm telling you, he's going to score a lot of goals in this league. You'll see."

I was standing with Artie, Mark Recchi, and Troy Loney. We were all just kind of looking at each other trying to figure out what was going on. This wasn't your normal behavior for a hockey coach during training camp, but as we'd find out, Bob Johnson wasn't your normal hockey coach nor person. I looked at Troy and said, "What the fuck is going on here? This is the NHL and our coach has a microphone in his hand. Are you serious? And look at him. He's having a blast."

I realized something about Badger Bob. Everything about him was real. Everything about him was the truth. Nothing was phony, he wasn't acting like this to get us to like him or for any other reason. It absolutely wasn't orchestrated. He was just so comfortable in his own skin. To this day, I've never seen anything like it. What we realized was that he loved hockey more than anyone else on the planet. We all loved the game. We still do. It was our passion, what we did for a living. But it was so much different with Badger Bob.

On the surface, he may have seemed like a strange fit for our team. Remember, we were a bunch of renegades. A bunch of cowboys. A bunch of daredevils. We were a bunch of drinkers, a bunch of carousers. We lived on the edge and we played the game on the edge. It's who we were as players and as people. Then along comes Bob Johnson, who was—and I say this affectionately—a little weird, a little quirky. A little different. He wasn't like us in any way. We knew it. But Bob just didn't care. He was going to be himself, and by the end of that training camp, we were really starting to like him. We found some kind of neutral ground. He was our coach, and after a few weeks, we realized that all the optimism wasn't bullshit. It was just Bob.

From Bob's standpoint, we must have been a fascinating team to coach. The talent was undeniable. Even though Mario's back was messed up and he wouldn't play until January that season, we were oozing with talent. Any coach in his right mind would have wanted to get his hands on that kind of talent. Artie and Rex were really starting to become stars. Johnny Cullen was becoming a star. We had Paul Coffey and Tommy Barrasso. Talent off the charts. But man, were we a pain in the ass.

I don't know how else to word it, so let's just put it this way: we had a bunch of party guys. Booze? Check. Gambling? You'd better believe it. I absolutely believe that, on the occasions back then when we played afternoon games, some of the players on our team were still drunk. And if you go back and look at some of the scores back then, you'll understand. We always had to play on New Year's Day—in the afternoon—in Washington. Got our asses kicked every year. I think we were somewhere between tipsy and hung over every single time. You'd be amazed by how it was back then. Nowadays, things are so different. I look at the modern-day Penguins and I see how they take care of their bodies. It's impressive to me and also kind of foreign, because in the late '80s and early '90s, it was a different world. I realize the way we were back then wouldn't fly in this era, but it's just who we were. We really didn't give a shit what anyone else thought about it, either. We were so unique. I think other great teams back then, like the Oilers and Islanders, probably had some of that in their personalities as well. We had talent. We were arrogant. We were cocky. We had this chip on our shoulder. It's who we were, and it was contagious. Put bluntly, we were a bunch of alpha males. Every damn one of us.

The funny thing is, this didn't seem to bother Bob the way it probably would have other coaches. Bob wasn't like us at all. I don't know if I ever heard him swear. I definitely never heard him say *fuck*. He just wasn't like that. How many hockey coaches don't use language like that? But not Bob. He was so different. And I'll tell you another thing that I grew to love about Bob: he never, ever tried to change our personalities. Not one bit. He was respectful and at ease with who we were, for better or worse. He literally never yelled at us. He never got angry at us. Never swore at us. I'm sure he got angry on occasion, but he never took it out on us. And the funny thing was, he didn't have to. Before Bob ever came into the room when we were playing like shit, we took care of it. We checked ourselves all the time. Bryan Trottier. Paul Coffey. Troy Loney. Artie Stevens. You've got to realize that about half of the guys in that locker room would go on to be captains at some point in their careers. It's incredible, really. One of those guys would always be holding us accountable for playing poorly. So, by the time Bob walked into the room, we'd already be yelling at each other. Bob would just walk in with that grin on his face and say, "Okay, boys. That period wasn't our best. But this one is going to be!"

It's amazing to me, when I think about it, just how perfect Bob was for us. We needed someone like him. We weren't the kind of people who responded well to someone yelling at us. That wasn't going to fly because we were too busy yelling at ourselves. We absolutely must have had more "fuck you" fights than any team in NHL history. It's all you ever heard on the bench. Cullen, Artie, and Rex were always "motherfucking" the defensemen for not getting them the puck quickly enough. The defensemen would yell right back at them. They'd yell back, "Fuck you. You aren't fucking open. Get fucking open and you'll get the puck."

And you know what? The coaches absolutely loved it. There was never one time when Bob, Rick Kehoe, or Barry Smith would say something like, "All right boys, let's come down a little bit here." Nah. Not at all. They loved it. They realized that we were a passionate group of people and that we were always going to be pushing ourselves. That whole staff was something. They had a great feel for the pulse of our team. They realized the best thing to do with us was simply step aside and let us figure things out. Think about it. How many coaches or coaching staffs would have interjected themselves into it? I'm thinking most people would have. And in that case, I'm telling you, it wouldn't have worked. Getting out of the way can be a very valuable attribute for a coaching staff and those guys were the masters. It was a unique environment, but we were a unique group of people. It became clear early on that in Bob Johnson, we finally had the coach we had been looking for.

It's amazing to think that Bob only coached us for one season, because we all learned so much from that man. At first, we didn't know what to make of him. Then, we started to like him and started to trust him. Pretty quickly after that, we realized we were in love with the guy, and it became a full romance. To this day, I've never known anyone who was as positive of a person as Badger Bob. And it's a good thing he was.

Not everything was going in the direction we wanted when camp opened. The big guy was hurt. Mario didn't play until January of that season. Remember, he came back against Buffalo in that last game, but we all knew he shouldn't have been playing. But that's the kind of man Mario is, and that's how hungry he was for a championship. He risked his health to go out there. Imagine that. Imagine playing in a National Hockey League game—and being the guy the other team is targeting physically all game—and being in so much pain that you couldn't tie your own skates. That was the situation Mario was in. In the summer of 1990, he opted to have surgery and then had to deal with a serious infection in his back. So even though we knew we had a lot of talent, we were without our best player and playing in the Patrick Division, which was hockey's best division. The Rangers were really building a good team. The Islanders had fallen off after their glory years but were still a threat. The Flyers were still very good and imposing, the Devils were a bitch to play against, and the Capitals had the best blue line in hockey. Yikes. And here we are, the Pittsburgh Penguins, who have never won a damn thing, not even a division title. So yeah, you can look at all the talent we had and all the future Hall of Famers and say, "Of course you guys were going to be great." But that wasn't the mindset at that time. I think it's important for everyone to understand that. When you're in the moment, when you're in the process of trying to be a championship team, you're not thinking it's going to be easy. It doesn't work like that. Instead, you're always pushing yourself and always wondering if you really are good enough. That's pretty much the position we were in entering that season. We knew we didn't suck, but we also knew we'd never won anything and that Mario was out indefinitely.

Badger Bob wasn't about to let us get down on ourselves, though. It wasn't his way. Right up until the season started, he was positive and making us feel like we were the greatest hockey team in the world. We had a tough assignment on opening night, as we had to travel to Washington. Believe it or not, we didn't always play well in Washington. That would change over the years, of course, but that wasn't an easy building to play in and the Capitals were a nasty team, very good defensively. So, what did we do there? We beat the hell out of them on opening night and big Artie scored four goals. What a way to start the season, and it was a sign of things to come.

And, you know, it's kind of funny. We didn't mind being without Mario. Especially by that season, we were used to it. You never knew from one day to the next if he was going to play. His back was really that bad. Sometimes, he wouldn't take warm-ups because the trainers were trying to fix him up. That's just the way it was with him. We had kind of an arrogance about us. Okay—we definitely had an arrogance about us. We weren't afraid to play without him. We almost welcomed the challenge.

Plus, we had a new wave of stars on that team. Artie was on the verge of becoming the best power forward in hockey. Mark Recchi was a real star. And then there was Johnny Cullen, the most underappreciated figure in Penguins history. Craig Patrick had added some serious veteran experience with guys like Bryan Trottier and Joey Mullen. It's not every day you add players like that to your team.

Things were going well in the regular season. We weren't a great team yet, but we were getting there. During the season, Craig traded for Larry Murphy. That's right, he added Trots, Joey, and Murph in about a five-month span. Seriously. All-time greats were coming in left and right—plus, we had drafted Jaromir Jagr earlier that year. We were cruising along and in playoff position. Mario was starting to hang out around the team more and more.

What a strange time it was for Mario. He was trying to do all these workouts and therapy to get his back into playing condition. It was a real struggle for him. Here's something I'll never forget. During this time, Mario had the weirdest smell about him. Seriously. He was taking some kind of medication at the time, and I don't know what it was called. It was something they were giving horses at the time. You could actually smell this medication on him. It made him sweat and it made him smell. It smelled like a combination of horse manure and wet garbage. Seriously. It was that bad. The smell just punched you right in the nose. I remember thinking, *What the hell is going on here? This poor guy.* When Mario's back was bad—and I think it was at its worst during that time—it was impossible not to feel bad for him. Mario was the type of guy who never really complained about anything. It's just who he was. He quietly sat there and dealt with all the pain, all the discomfort. It was awful for us to watch, but he was so tough about it. He never said a word about the pain. But I'm telling you, the look on his face told a completely different story. He was in agony the whole time. For the rest of my life, I'll never forget the look on his face during that time. He was being tortured by all that back pain. The poor guy just wanted to play hockey. Imagine being the very best in the world at what you do and not being able to function properly because you're in so much pain. That's the way it was for him.

However, Mario got better, slowly but surely. By the end of January, he was back. True to form, he put up three helpers in his first game back in Quebec. We were home to the Capitals in our next game, and Mario scored a dramatic goal late in the contest to tie it. Of course he did. He always had a flair for the dramatic that was a little bit different than anyone else's.

Still, Mario being back didn't fix all our flaws. We still weren't good defensively and we didn't play great in February. We had a tendency to sit back and let Mario take care of everything when he was in the lineup, but hockey doesn't work that way. Even the greatest player in the game needs some help. It is the ultimate team sport. And oh boy, did Craig get us some help in March.

Right before the trade deadline, Craig swung the biggest deal in team history. We sent Johnny Cullen, Zarley Zalapski, and Jeff Parker to the Hartford Whalers for Ron Francis, Ulf Samuelsson, and Grant Jennings. Fucking wow. History will tell you that we won that trade in a big way. Some people even think Eddie Johnston, who was the general manager of the Whalers at that time, was doing his old team a favor. Nothing could be further from the truth and, at the time, many observers thought the Whalers actually won that trade.

Zalapski was a big-time talent, but this was really about Cullen. He had become a leader on our team and was a top-five scorer at the time of the trade. He was a legitimately good No. 1 center in the NHL at that point and, if he was the No. 2 center behind Mario, then you really had something. We had a serious problem, though. We didn't play defense. We didn't really know how. We weren't always that interested, either. It just wasn't our thing. The more goals the better. That's how we liked to play the game. This was the trade that absolutely changed everything, especially because of Ronnie. No center in the league played defense like Ronnie, and he was still a prolific offensive player to boot. I can't imagine a better center to play behind Mario, and as sad as I was to see Cullen leave, I knew it was the right trade after the fact. You had to ask yourself some questions: Could Johnny kill penalties like Ronnie? Could Johnny win draws like Ronnie could? Could Johnny run a power play like Ronnie could? Could Johnny shut down the other team's best players the way Ronnie could? Cullen was having an unbelievable season. He was a close friend of mine and everyone else's, and he was just a hell of a hockey player. The fact of the matter is, though, that he couldn't bring a lot of elements to the table that Ronnie could. It was a gutsy trade. We were giving up a lot. But we were bringing players who provided a defensive element, and that was something that we knew we badly needed.

Ronnie, Ulfie, and Grant Jennings all put defense first. It was a huge deal for us at that time.

Four things really started to happen in March. Mario was back and he was flying. If you watched the Penguins then, you remember. If you didn't, well, he would just get this look on his face. You could tell he was feeling better. And he was so hungry. It was go time. The trade had changed us in a good way. We were finally a balanced hockey team. Additionally, as a group, we were coming together and developing a serious amount of confidence. We were starting to gain on the Rangers for the division lead. And Jagr was becoming a star.

It's easy to forget how young Jagr was. He turned 19 in February of that season, for God's sake. But the talent was just off the charts. He was from Czechoslovakia, and a lot of teams were afraid to draft players from there because it had been a communist country. He should have been the top pick that year, even though it was a very good draft, with guys like Owen Nolan, Petr Nedved (who had already defected), Keith Primeau, Mike Ricci. That's a good draft and you can't be critical of any of those choices. But come on. Jagr was such an awesome talent, and it's obvious he was the best player in that draft (although a goalie named Martin Brodeur wasn't so bad, either).

Craig wasn't afraid to draft a player from Jagr's situation. And from the beginning of camp, you could see that he was special. I've never seen such a strong young player. We all knew he was going to become a superstar. That said, he was still a kid and a little immature. You know about all the speeding tickets and all the KIT KAT bars, which, along with the ladies of Pittsburgh, became his favorite things. What you might not know is something that happened during a game against the Devils that season.

Jags didn't like being yelled at. He was totally sensitive. It's just his personality. Bob and the other coaches were always, always warning him about skating with his head down through the neutral zone. Always. But Jags didn't listen. Like most great players, he possessed this unique ability to avoid big hits, even if he wasn't looking. He didn't need to see other players. He could just feel the game. You never saw Mario get lit up. You never saw Gretzky get lit up. It's because of the feel they have, the feel other players can only dream of.

But one night against the Devils, Jags got absolutely lit up. I was playing on his line at the time. When we got back to the bench, the coaches started yelling at him. I was sitting beside him on the bench, and they were just letting him hear it. I noticed something felt a little off.

I looked over at Jags, and the poor kid was crying. I'm not talking a little tear rolling down his cheek. I mean, he was flat-out crying uncontrollably. He was having trouble breathing he was crying so hard. He just couldn't handle the criticism. So, at this point, I don't know what to do. My linemate is crying his eyes out and we had to go back out on the ice. Then things got even worse. At the far end of the bench, Artie noticed that Jags was crying. Now, please understand, I love Artie. He is literally one of my favorite people and one of my favorite teammates of all time. We're both from Boston

In 1990, "Badger" Bob Johnson was exactly what the Penguins needed. (Getty Images)

and have always been friends. You'll never hear me say a bad word about Artie. But at that moment, I truly wish Artie wouldn't have seen Jags crying, because it just made a bad situation worse.

"Bourquey," I heard Artie scream. "Is he crying?"

This made Jags cry even harder, of course. I don't know what would have to happen to get Artie to cry during a hockey game, but he wasn't amused. I just put my arm around Jags. I kept saying, "It's okay, Jags. It's okay. Let's go have a great shift. It's no big deal. Everything is going to be all right." He finally settled down, but that was a hell of a thing, to say the least. But man, what a hockey player. We all knew, even when he was a teenager, that he would be the guy who one day would replace Mario as hockey's greatest player. We knew it immediately. He had everything. And even if he was a little immature, he had this habit of stepping up in the biggest of moments. He was in such incredible shape, he always scored a ton of goals in the third period. He was never afraid of the big moments, either. Not even when he was a kid. Maybe a coach yelling at him scared him, but nothing about hockey did.

With the amazing trade Craig pulled off, Mario being healthy, Jagr coming of age, and the entire team starting to believe, we got hot. Hotter than hell. And we were breathing down the Rangers' necks.

On St. Patrick's Day, we rolled into the Garden and beat the hell out of them. Mario had a big day. We were feeling it. A couple nights later, we hosted the Rangers and the game went to overtime. Artie got the game-winner. It was a crazy goal. He threw the puck into New York territory, it bounced off the back wall, and somehow caromed off John Vanbiesbrouck and into the goal by a couple of inches. We were all slowly starting to believe that something special was happening.

We finally clinched our first division championship with a victory in Detroit. It was symbolic, I suppose, that Mario didn't play that night. He had an eye injury and was out for a few days. We had grown so much together as a team that we clinched that first division title even without him, which I think said something about the talent and character we had. But I'm so glad Mario was behind the bench that night. He stood with the coaches, with a patch protecting his eye, and was there for the celebration. He deserved to take part in it. After all, there are no Pittsburgh Penguins without Mario Lemieux. It was that way in 1991, and it's still that way today.

CHAPTER 8
THE SPRING
OF SPRINGS

The 1991 playoffs began against the New Jersey Devils. We were better than them and we knew it, but we knew this series wasn't going to be easy. There was something about them that irritated us. They were a real bitch to play against. This was before the days of Martin Brodeur and before the days of them trapping you continuously. But they were still strong defensively and really gave us fits. They took Game 1 at the Igloo. We didn't play well. In Game 2, we weren't much better. But we managed to get the game into overtime, and Jagr scored one of the great goals of his career to even the series. I was playing on a line with Jags and Bryan Trottier then. Two Hall of Famers on our line...not bad, right? Jagr swooped through the Devils and made an incredible play to beat Chris Terreri.

The series went back and forth. We split the next two games in Jersey, but then we lost Game 5 at home. So we had to go to Jersey and win just to force a Game 7. Making matters worse, Tommy Barrasso got hurt in Game 5 and wasn't available for the rest of the series.

We had a lot of baggage at that point in time. Remember, we hadn't won anything. And yeah, we had talent, but lots of teams with talent never win anything in the NHL. We knew that, and we were fearful. The way our season ended the year before was still fresh in our minds. We knew we were one more loss away from the same fate. It was still hanging around our locker room, that awful fear of losing. We had people on our team who feared losing more than they loved winning. But in retrospect, I think this is where all the new guys came into play. Guys like Trots, Ronnie, Murphy, Ulfie, they weren't on that team the year before. They weren't impacted by it the way some of us were. We really relied on them when we were down to the Devils. Some people in the locker room said some things before Game 6. Trots would always get up and talk. We listened when he talked, let me tell you.

We were in for a battle. The Devils were nasty. Laurie Boschman was a prick to play against. John MacLean, total asshole to play against. Those Russian guys on their team were all dicks to play against. Claude Lemieux was as dirty as it got, and he could really play.

We went up early in Game 6. Artie was playing an incredible game, as he always did when we were in trouble in a series. Things were going well. But then the Devils had a power play, and boy did I ever fuck up. Peter Stastny was my guy on a rotation. And I missed him. Randy Hillier and Peter Taglianetti were out there too. They rotated and I was supposed to rotate down, but I never made it down there. Stastny was wide open and had an empty net.

Then came what we like to call "The Save." Frankie Pietrangelo, who was playing in place of Tommy, made a glove save for the ages. It's the greatest save I've ever seen, one of the greatest saves in hockey history. After the save, I just looked up to the heavens, then I skated up to Frankie and said, "Great fucking save." I really didn't know what else to say.

But think about it. Every team that's won the Cup had a Frankie moment. Wendell Young, our third-string goalie, was huge. He kept the guys loose. All that work ethic. You need certain people to win the Cup. The Oilers. The Hawks. The Islanders. All the best dynasties will tell you that you need those kinds of guys.

Game 6 was a war. The Devils had a controversial goal disallowed. It wasn't a comfortable game for us, but we held on for the 4–3 win.

Two nights later at the Igloo, the Devils didn't stand a chance. Playing in a must-win game like in Game 6, and finding a way to win it, really did something for our confidence.

Jiri Hrdina scored twice in Game 7 and Frankie pitched a shutout in a 4–0 win. I remember the sense of relief we had after that game. We all took a deep breath because we knew we had been in trouble. But once we escaped that series, a confidence became evident. We were feeling good about ourselves.

Then the Capitals kicked the shit out of us in Game 1. That spring, we would play in Game 1 at home three times and lose all three. We didn't win a Game 1 at all that spring—and got soundly beaten in all of them to boot. Coincidence? Nah. Not at all.

We didn't lose Game 1 on purpose, of course. But I think something subconscious was going on, to be quite honest with you. We were so cocky, you know? We liked the idea of people thinking we were in trouble. We liked the idea of people writing us off. We liked the idea that we could actually flip that magical switch. Not many teams could flip that switch, but we could. And we knew it. So yeah, we lost Game 1 of a series again. Big deal. Our mindset was basically, *We're down in the series. You think you've got us. You think we're in trouble. Now we're going to kick your ass. Suck on that.*

It wasn't that simple in the next game, though. It was a wild, back-and-forth affair with the Capitals in Game 2. Late in the game, they were ahead 6–5. I couldn't believe it. We were in serious trouble. Go down 2–0, and your series is in trouble, especially when you lose those first two games at home. Then, something amazing happened.

I'm on the bench. We're down a goal late and it's about time to pull the goaltender. Tommy skates to the bench. We had some tired players on the ice at the time, and everyone got a little confused for a second. I think we froze. I think the coaches froze. So, the play was in the offensive zone when Tommy came to the bench. The only problem was, no one knew who the extra attacker would be. We had some of our big guns on the ice, of course. But no one knew whose turn it was to jump onto the ice. I'm sitting there trying to figure out what the hell is going on. Then, all of a sudden, Randy Gilhen just jumps on the ice. That's right; Randy Gilhen. Randy scored 55 career goals in 11 seasons. He wasn't a bad player, but he was a defensive-minded guy, a good faceoff guy. One thing about him was that he was always in the game. Some guys sit there on the bench, not playing a ton, and as a result they're not focused. They're not into the game. It happened a lot back then. But Randy was different. He was a thinking man's hockey player. Always paying attention. Honestly, he was one of those guys who would never shut up on the bench. Ever. And you know what? In that moment, it was a good thing he was into the game and so in tune with everything.

After everyone froze for a second, I can remember hearing Badger yell "Center! Center!" By then, though, Randy was already jumping on the ice. He just said to himself, "Fuck it, I'll go." A few seconds later, Randy charged toward the net and scored on a backhand shot. That was divine intervention from the Good Lord above. I'm convinced of it. God decided Randy was going to score the biggest goal of his life at that moment, and so he did. It was bizarre. But it was special, and I'll never forget it. The place went absolutely bonkers, and, in overtime, Ronnie Francis set up Artie Stevens on a two on one and Artie buried it. The series was tied and the Capitals never recovered.

We beat the hell out of them in the next three games. They never changed their approach. They loved to play the dump-and-chase game. Problem was, Tommy was the best goalie in the league at handling the puck. He loved it. So Washington would dump the puck into our territory, and Tommy would just dump it back out. He made it look so easy. Their tactic never had a chance. Rex and Artie got hot. And then there was Mario. He was awesome in that series, and you could see him getting more and more comfortable. He was starting to take over. We put away the Capitals in five in what was the easiest series that spring. For the first time in Penguins history, we had made it to a conference title. And I was going home to Boston.

I'll never forget the spring of 1991. I was already in love with the city of Pittsburgh at that point, but something changed during that run. Pittsburgh truly became a hockey town during that spring. I remember driving everywhere in the city that spring, and all you saw were Penguins sweaters and Penguins signs in front yards. It was everywhere. You couldn't go anywhere that spring without people wanting to talk about hockey and letting us know how much they were supporting us. Pittsburgh is not only a great sports town, but it's a town of champions. We knew this. The Pirates were excellent then, with Barry Bonds and some other talented players. They had won two World Series in the 1970s and were still No. 2 in Pittsburgh behind the Steelers. Both franchises had last won championships in the 1979 season. So it had been almost a dozen years since Pittsburgh had tasted a championship. While our play was appreciated and our fan base was clearly growing rapidly, we felt the pressure. This was Pittsburgh. Getting to the final four? Big deal. Win the whole damn thing if you want to go down as Pittsburgh legends. The city was behind us, though. These fans were so hungry for a championship and we badly wanted to oblige them. It was starting to consume the city, and that did motivate us.

With all due respect to the fans that fill PPG Paints Arena these days, the fans back then were a little different, a little more raucous. That was a blue-collar crowd. The Igloo smelled a little like booze and cigarette smoke on some nights. If you looked around back then, you didn't see any suits in the crowd. You didn't see any rich people. And that crowd was right the hell on top of you. It was an intimidating environment for other teams, and for us it was absolutely perfect. Everything was starting to come together on the team and in the city. What a special time it was.

We started the Wales Conference Final in Boston, a place we rarely enjoyed success. The Boston Garden was a real problem for us. It was as small as you've probably heard. The corners were shallow. It was a shoebox. They built their team to thrive in that building. They were big, physical, and nasty. For us, it was a terrible place to play. We were all about skill and speed, and it was difficult to showcase those attributes in that building. Plus, it was the most miserable building for a visiting team. I never played well there when I was younger, probably for a lot of reasons—one of which was how damn hot I always was. They had baseboard heating in that place. It was May when the series started, and it was a warm spring—to the tune of 80 degrees outside. What did the Bruins do? They cranked the heat all the way up in the visitor's room. It was unbearable. It literally felt like a sauna. In Game 1, most of our guys had to stand outside in the hallway during intermissions because it was literally too hot to function in the dressing room. We couldn't stand it. Also, how I didn't catch some kind of disease in the showers there is a minor miracle. The health department should have closed the damn place down. It was seriously that bad.

But it motivated us. It motivated us in a big way—just not in Game 1, of course. Yeah, we got clobbered again in Game 1. Same old story. But we were more than ready for Game 2, and we played a great game. Mario scored twice in the third period to put us ahead 4–3. Then, Dan Marouelli, the referee that night, put us down two men late in the third period. I couldn't believe it. We were already shorthanded, and he put Taglianetti in the box. It was bullshit. You have to understand that, back then, penalties weren't really called in the playoffs. Putting a team down two men late in the third period of a close game was unheard of. We were furious. The Bruins tied the game. Then Rosey Ruzicka won the game for the Bruins in overtime. I was so pissed. We all were. We knew we were the better team that night and that we deserved the win. We were all frustrated, but Artie took things to another level.

I took a shower and was about to go outside to see my family. As I was getting dressed, I looked over and noticed Artie was surrounded by a large number of reporters. They were coming in waves. Artie was wearing a white dress shirt and he was just sweating right through that shirt, it was so hot in there. But he wanted everyone to know something. He kept repeating over and over again, "We're going to win four straight. We're going to win this series. I guarantee it." I can still hear that deep, baritone voice of his booming. He wanted the whole world to know. He took the time to tell every single reporter.

My first thought was, *What the hell, Artie?*

I couldn't believe he said it. No one made predictions back then. I think he was the second person ever to make such a prediction, behind Joe Namath. This was before Mark Messier did it, before anyone was doing it. Before I got on the plane, I saw Troy Loney. Man, do I love Troy. Troy, Bob Errey, and I had been with the Penguins the longest, along with Mario. There was a bond there. I went over to Troy before we got on the plane and I said, "Hey, Troy, did you hear what Artie just said to all the reporters?"

Troy looked at me and said, "Good. I'm glad he said it, because we are going to win this series."

I thought about it for a moment. I took it all in. Then I looked back at Troy and said, "Fucking right we are."

In retrospect, it was one of the most important moments in franchise history. We were the Penguins. We hadn't ever won a damn thing. I'll never forget standing there in that awful locker room, hearing Artie let the world know the Pittsburgh Penguins weren't going to be pushed around anymore. It was very calculated. He knew exactly what he was doing. He was from Boston. He grew up a Bruins fan. He knew exactly what he was doing. If you're going to talk the talk, you better walk the walk. Mario was great, the best player ever. We had so much talent on that team. But in that series, at that very moment, Artie was our leader. We followed him. He took his game to a different place the rest of the series. I can still see him walking into the locker room during that series, the confidence he had. Man. Those words were real. He wasn't saying it for attention or to get a rise out of anyone. He said it because he meant it. We would have followed him right through a wall during that series. He was truly one of my favorite teammates ever, no doubt about it. The way he walked and the way he played that spring; man, that was special. There was something different about him. He wasn't about to let us fail.

Game 3 gave us one of the more famous moments in Penguins history. Ulfie took out Cam Neely with a nasty hit. Was it dirty? Yeah, it was. Was there contact to Cam's knee? Yeah, there was. I don't remember all the details, but I think he had a freak injury during that time aside from the hit. It was a nasty hit, a charley-horse hit. Was he trying to give him a charley horse? Sure. But the whole thing happened so quickly. I can assure you that Ulfie wasn't trying to end the guy's career or anything like that. It wasn't a blindside hit. He just threw his knee out there.

Well, Neely was hurt, and Boston coach Mike Milbury went absolutely insane. He had a stick in his hands and was banging it on the boards to alert the referee that he wanted to talk. He looked like a kid throwing a fit. Then, Mario roofed on a shot on a breakaway not long after, Artie scored a big goal, and we won comfortably 4–1. All of a sudden, we felt good about ourselves. Then, Milbury opened his mouth.

This guy called Bob Johnson the "Professor of Goonism" in the press the next day. I'll never forget it. Understand that, by this time, we loved Bob as though he were our father. Seriously. That's how close we had become with him. And honestly, we didn't think much of Milbury after that comment. For him to suggest that Bob was telling Ulfie to go after Neely was ridiculous. Don't get me wrong; we were being physical with their best players. Bobby Errey just lit up Ray Bourque all series long. Ulfie was going after Neely all series long. Well, let me ask you something: Do you think the Bruins were going after Mario every chance they got? Of course they were. It was far worse than anything we were doing to their big guns. We didn't think much of Milbury, but we weren't calling him a goon or anything like that. This was straight gasoline on the fire. We already had the bonfire going because of what Artie had said after Game 2. But for Milbury to say that shit about our ice general; oh man, we were so angry.

In Game 4, we had another easy win. It was 4–1 again and it was never in doubt. We had been the better team for three straight games and we knew it. We traveled back to Boston and felt great about ourselves.

The Bruins never had a chance in Game 5. We kicked the hell out of them 7–2. Artie had a hat trick. It was one of the great wins in franchise history. It was like, *Holy shit, did that just happen?* I think that was the moment when we knew. Oh, we respected the Bruins, and we knew the series wasn't over. But when we went there and beat them like that in their building, I believe that was the moment I knew we had a real chance to win the Stanley Cup. We could all feel it.

Game 6. May 11, 1991. Saturday night in the 'Burgh. It was a beautiful day, and the city was so hungry. Win that night and we're in the Final against the North Stars, who we knew we could beat.

The Bruins went up early 2–0. We were a little tight, and they had been in this position before. They weren't afraid. But we started to get back into it. Mario set up Murph to get us back into the game. Then Mario gave me a set-up I'll never forget.

In the second period, I was in front of the net when Ray Bourque knocked me on my ass. I was out there playing with Mario and Rex. Again, me out there with two Hall of Famers. What's going on here? But I wasn't complaining. So, I was on the ice, but I got up quickly. Rex threw one toward the net. Mario was in the neighborhood, but he was completely tied up, so there was nothing he could do. I got to the puck and I was about to do something stupid—maybe an impossible pass or an attempt to stickhandle around someone. I don't know what I was going to do, but I can tell you that the last thing on my mind was shooting the puck. I wasn't an idiot, though, so I did exactly what I was told. The Igloo was a loud place, but it wasn't so loud that I couldn't hear Mario bark out instructions. When the puck touched my blade, I distinctly heard Mario yell, "Shoot it!" I didn't have time to overthink the situation. When Mario tells you to shoot the puck, you shoot the puck. I didn't pick a corner or anything, but I fired a puck at Andy Moog and, somehow, it got through him and helped us even the game. Trust me, I was about to try something cute in that situation. Mario was such a genius, though, and was so locked in at that point in time. Everything he said and did was right. Everything. If Mario said shoot it, you're damn right I was going to shoot it. I'll never forget hearing him through the crowd.

It reminded me of a time, a few years earlier, when I played with Mario for the first time. We had never been on a line before and, of course, I started my career as a defenseman. I was a forward by the late '80s and, one night, in the middle of a game, the coaches yelled out that I was on Mario's line. Mario could immediately see that I was totally terrified to play a shift with him. You must understand, Mario had total Spidey Sense. He really did. So, he looked at me and knew how nervous I was. He slid down the bench to sit with me before we took the ice. He looked at me and said, "Bourquey, it's okay. Just go to the net. And when you go to the net, make sure you lean really hard on your stick."

Simple and to the point. Straightforward. I liked it. So, we took our shift. I was flying down the left wing. Mario had the puck and entered the zone down the right wing. He hit the brakes around the hash marks and pulled up. I was driving to the post with a defenseman on my shoulder. Then, I remembered what to do. Lean on your stick. So that's precisely what I did. I never really saw the puck at that moment. I was so busy doing what the big guy said to do. Suddenly, the puck literally bounced off my stick and went into the net. I couldn't believe it. He just had a little grin on his face. He literally did things like that for fun with new linemates. He was that good, and I honestly think the game bored him at times, because he could do anything he wanted. Mario enjoyed challenges like that. The point is, you always listened to him when he spoke.

Game 6 went back and forth. Gordie Roberts put us ahead, but with Tommy stranded away from the net, the Bruins tied it later in the third. But then Rex showed up, as he always did in big games. He was shot out of a cannon that night. It was unreal. He had this competitive nature that made him stand out, even in the biggest of games in the world's greatest league. Rex went flying down the right wing and buried a wrist shot past Moog. The place went wild.

Mario ended it with an empty-netter. He fell to his knees when the puck went in. I was on the ice when the game ended and skated right up to Tommy to give him a hug. Just a couple of Boston kids going to the Stanley Cup Final after beating the Bruins. Wow. Just wow. In the handshake line, Kenny Hodge Jr. took my hand and said, "Bourquey, great game." That meant a lot to me. We knew each other from Boston. I looked at him and said, "This is one of the greatest games I've ever been a part of."

Up to that point, it was the greatest moment in Penguins history. By a mile. They brought out the Wales Conference Trophy—but it was just there for show, right? Teams never touched it back then. But we didn't give a shit. Remember, we were who we were. Cowboys. Rebels. Riverboat gamblers. Wild men. Alpha men. So, Mario picked up that fucking trophy and took it for a twirl. Then a few other guys carried it around the ice. We didn't care if people had a problem with us doing that. It didn't matter to us at all. We had never won anything in Pittsburgh and we weren't about to let some stupid tradition change how we operated. It was a pretty wild night in the city. We were four wins away from hoisting the Cup, with only the North Stars standing in our way.

CHAPTER 9
OUR DATE WITH DESTINY

Heading into the 1991 Stanley Cup Final, we respected the North Stars but definitely felt like we were the better team. They made the playoffs with a sub-.500 record and, somehow, got hotter than hell and pulled off a bunch of upsets in the playoffs. When the series began on May 15, we were feeling good about ourselves. Really good.

Then, of course, we lose Game 1. Our fans were upset, but we really weren't. Honestly, we were so comfortable in that position. We probably wouldn't have known what to do if we had won the first game of a series. But we had an issue in all those Game 1 losses: we gave up a ton of goals. We played a loose game defensively and lost 5–4. We fell into bad habits early in all those series. It was our instinct just to see how many goals we could score and, quite honestly, that was good enough on a lot of nights. There's firepower, and then there's the kind of firepower we could produce. Only when we got in trouble did we really start to bear down defensively.

Game 2 was a different story and gave us the greatest goal of Mario's career. I'm proud to say I assisted on it, even if I made the degree of difficulty a little greater. We were up 2–1 in the second period, but the North Stars were starting to press us. We weren't comfortable just yet. And even though we absolutely thought we were the better team, we couldn't lose that game. Fall down 2–0 with the first two games at home and you're pretty much screwed.

Tommy made a save and the puck caromed off his pads, like always. You always had to be aware of that with Tommy. His pads were a little different, and off them, it was like the puck was pretty much bouncing off boards. So, I corralled the rebound. Then, I heard a noise. I knew exactly what that noise meant. The big guy wanted the puck.

Mario had different kinds of yells, and we all knew them. Normally, he would give you a certain yell. It was his way of telling you, "You have time, just give me a crisp pass." That was the ordinary

Mario yell. But every now and then, you'd get a different one. It was more of a loud yip. Short. Loud. More direct. That's when you knew to get him the fucking puck. So, I heard this noise, and, even though we were in our own territory, I knew to give him the puck as quickly as possible. I only needed to hear it once. It was different than any noise I had ever heard him make on the ice. He really, really wanted this puck. So, what did I do? I got him the puck. It wasn't a good pass. In fact, I never looked at him. I had a feel for where he was, so I just delivered it in his direction. Remember, Mario had the longest reach of just about anyone who ever played, so I knew if I got the puck somewhere in the 412 area code, he was going to be fine. I just threw it in his direction. The pass was well behind him, but it didn't matter. He never even broke stride. He reached back and gathered the puck. It didn't matter that the pass I threw him was a grenade that was almost out of reach. What happened next was hockey history. I was on my way to the bench after I made the pass, but I paused for a second and got a good look at what happened, because I knew he was about to do something special. He never disappointed you in that way. I don't know what it was, and I actually don't think he could even tell you why those moments popped up. But every now and then, Mario just felt like putting on a show. I truly believe he had no control over it. For whatever reason, it just happened organically. That was one of those moments. He was absolutely flying through the neutral zone and two defensemen were left in his way, Neil Wilkinson and Shawn Chambers. Those poor bastards never had a chance. Earlier in the game, Mario had a similar rush and they shut him down. It wasn't about to happen twice. He put the puck right between Chambers' legs and blew through both of them. Then, for reasons I'll never understand, Jon Casey tried to poke check Mario. He kept trying to do it all series. Good luck. Mario went to the backhand and that was that. Never in my life have I, nor will I ever again, see a goal like that. Time stood still for just a moment. On the bench, all we could do was laugh and say, "Holy shit." That's it. We had nothing else to say.

Everyone has their favorite Mario goal, and there have been so many:

- The day in Quebec when he carried players on his back and scored
- The day he saved our season in overtime in Washington in 1988
- Going between Ray Bourque's legs and beating Andy Moog
- The Game 1 winner in 1992 against the Hawks
- His breakaway against the Flyers in 1997 in what we thought was his last home shift
- The Canada Cup clincher in 1987

Hell, there are hundreds of others to pick from, because no one scored highlight-reel goals like the big guy. Not even close. But that goal was special, both for the remarkable athleticism it required and because of the timing. Game 2, Stanley Cup Final. It's a close game, we're in a little bit of trouble, and we desperately need to win. And he pulls off a goal like that. Give me a break.

At that moment, I truly believed we were going to win that series, and I wasn't alone. We all believed it. If we were playing a powerful team from the Campbell Conference like the Blackhawks or Oilers, it would have been a different story. But we knew we were better than Minnesota.

Of course, there was always some drama associated with us. Game 3 was back in Minnesota, and Mario wasn't on the bench when the game started. His back had gone out on him. Now, this was pretty typical. It happened all the time, in fact. His back was always a problem, and, on many occasions, he didn't take the morning skate or the pregame skate. But more often than not, the trainers would get him loosened up to the point that he could play. Mario at 50 percent was still better than anyone else, so we weren't so worried. About five minutes into the game, there was still no Mario. We kind of looked and said, "Oh shit. He's not coming out tonight." And he didn't. We lost the game 3–1. We didn't play poorly, but it wasn't in the cards on that night. No big deal, though. I wouldn't say we were rattled or anything like that. We knew Mario would probably be good for Game 4 and we had been down like this before. But then we got pissed.

The next day, all these stories come out about the North Stars planning their parade route in the Twin Cities. Seriously. The Twins had won the World Series in 1987 and they were talking having about a similar parade. Chris Dahlquist was a very humble guy and a former Penguin. He was on the North Stars then, and even he made some comments about the parade route. I couldn't believe it. I was totally stunned. We weren't the kind of group who was impacted very often by a little trash talk. Whatever. We really didn't mind that kind of stuff. But I can honestly tell you that this situation totally offended us. It really did. So, after practice the next day, what happens? Bryan Trottier literally takes the article about the parade and tapes it on the wall in our locker room. Guys were talking about their championship rings and all this crap. You want to anger Mario Lemieux? Ron Francis? Paul Coffey? Kevin Stevens? Mark Recchi? Joey Mullen? Larry Murphy? Jaromir Jagr? Tommy Barrasso? Come on. Be smarter than that.

As you may have imagined, we came out absolutely flying in Game 4. Before you knew it, we were up 3–0. Mario scored an early goal and he was on fire. Things were looking up. But I had to go down to save the day.

The North Stars came back—I guess you could say that protecting leads wasn't our strong suit. We were clinging to a 4–3 lead in the third period when Troy Loney got tagged for a five-minute high-sticking penalty. Mark Tinordi acted like he was dead, but there was blood, and that's all it took for a five-minute major. For the first 3:30, we were awesome. It was a coming-of-age moment for us. We were actually playing defense. Everyone was doing an unbelievable job on the penalty kill. Then I decided to take matters into my own hands. Casey went behind the net to play the puck, and I was nearby. I took the biggest dive ever, and the ref called it. Power play over. So was the game. Casey didn't really say anything to me. Once upon a time, we played in Baltimore, and we were pretty good friends. He understood the situation. He shouldn't even have taken the chance, and he knew I was going to try and draw one. It was the best kill in Penguins history, and I'd like to say it was one of the better flops in Penguins history, too. I just kind of looked at Casey and shrugged my shoulders. I had a feeling I was going to get that call because, quite honestly, I had a great relationship with the referees. I was a nervous player. So, so nervous. I couldn't sleep the night before games. I was always talking with everyone just to calm my anxiety. I literally never shut up. Teammates. Coaches. Other players. And the refs. I was always talking with the refs. So, the refs usually liked me. I don't think they particularly liked our team, because we had a bunch of mouthy guys and, frankly, we made it difficult for refs. We were so talented that we were drawing penalties constantly. Mario and Jagr couldn't be legally defended one-on-one. They just couldn't. But it's not like refs were going to give us 10 power plays a game, so there was always some friction there. But I got along with those guys perfectly well, so they didn't mind me flopping every now and then. I'll never regret that one. We held on for the win, and the series was headed back to Pittsburgh.

We were unstoppable in the first period of Game 5. Mario had a goal and two assists before the first period was even over. He was our leader, and by then, he could smell it. When you're starting to take control of a series, it's kind of like surgery. You are surgically removing the heart of that team. That's what Mario did in that series. They just knew he was better. The North Stars had no one remotely close to his league and, deep down, I think they realized, when push came to shove, they had no answer for all his magic. From the first shift of Game 4, when he was back in the lineup, he just overwhelmed the North Stars. And believe me when I tell you that we fed off it. This game was so similar to Game 4. We took a huge lead, then we had to hold on. But we did what we had to do, and suddenly, we were one victory away from destiny.

I'll never forget that crowd that night. We never did clinch a Cup at home. That night was the closest we ever came. The crowd was just bonkers, and I must admit I often find myself missing the way crowds were back then. It was an old-school, blue-collar Pittsburgh kind of crowd. When you heard the crowd going crazy even before a game, you pretty much knew you weren't going to lose. It was a special time to be a hockey fan in Pittsburgh.

It was a special time to be a member of the Pittsburgh Penguins, too. Because we were on our way.

CHAPTER 10
MAY 25, 1991

The day after Game 5, a Friday, we headed back to Minneapolis. It's funny, the things you remember. Back then, we were still flying commercially in the regular season and in the first round. Usually by the time you got to the second round, teams started taking care of you with chartered flights. I remember our flight back to the Twin Cities well. There was this quiet confidence about us that day. Usually we were a noisy bunch, but not on that day. We weren't afraid. I don't even know if we were nervous. Probably a little bit. But we were quiet. The usual card games were being played, but everyone was all business on that day.

My roommate that season was big Jay Caufield. I couldn't have asked for a better guy to room with. He was an enforcer and didn't really see time in the playoffs. But he was the most supportive teammate you could possibly imagine. On that flight to Minnesota, I couldn't stop thinking about Jay. And Jock Callender. Guys like that. We had a bunch of stars on that team. We had good role players too, guys like me, Bob Errey, Troy Loney. We had been around a long time and we felt like we had earned a championship. But man, I was thinking about other guys on that flight. The healthy scratches. The guys who barely got a chance to play at the NHL level. Those guys always worked so hard to make sure they were game ready, just in case. And they kept us sharp at all times. You don't get that close to winning a championship without the guys behind the scenes. All I could think about on that flight was winning one for guys like Jay. I didn't want to let him down. I didn't want to let any of the them down. That team was different than any group in which I'd ever played. We were truly a family at that point, from Craig and Bob all the way down.

I didn't sleep much that night. I was a horrible sleeper in general, especially before games. I was hooked on Halcion, which was like Ambien back then. It was nasty shit, though. People in other countries were sleepwalking and killing people in their sleep, crazy stuff like that. It all went back to my nerves, my anxiety. Back then, if I could get two straight hours of sleep without waking up, I was so happy. I learned to function on sleep deprivation during most of my playing career, especially during the playoffs.

After the morning skate, I did something a little strange. I found a church. I'll have you know that the Penguins have won five championships in their history, and no matter where I was on that particular day—Minneapolis, Chicago, Detroit, San Jose, Nashville—I found a church and I prayed. That's how much being a Pittsburgh Penguin has always meant to me. It seemed like a good idea to make sure the big man upstairs was on our side on those nights.

We had our morning skate in Bloomington. I was in our hotel lobby, and then I decided to find a church. And I remember how well I slept that day. It was incredible. My go-to sleeping time on game days was usually from 2:00 to 4:00 PM, and that's exactly what I did on that day. I slept like a baby. It was the best I had slept in ages. I think part of it was this internal confidence I was feeling. Deep down, I knew there wasn't going to be a Game 7 in Pittsburgh. No way. It was our time, and I could feel this peace that I had never felt before. Right to my inner core. I had no doubt we were going to win that hockey game.

The locker room before the game was incredible. The killer instinct in that room cut like a knife. We were a great mix of younger guys who were so damn hungry for that Cup and a few veterans who had been there and already won it. It was so perfect. The pregame mood in that locker room was something I'll never forget. A few guys got up and spoke before we took the ice. It was the guys you'd assume: Bryan Trottier, Kevin Stevens. Mario was our leader, and Ronnie Francis was an incredible leader. Paul Coffey, too. But our vocal leaders were Trots and Artie. I'm sure they were nervous just like anyone else would have been. Even Trots, who had already won the Cup four times with the Islanders. But he knew he had to say something to us before we took the ice. He wanted to. You could see it. Some guys looked nervous and probably didn't want to talk. Not everyone is cut out for speaking in moments like those. But Trots and Artie said what needed to be said. They did everything just right. We were pretty much ready to run through a wall when we took the ice, but there was a certain calm about us, too. Our heads were on straight. We were fired up but totally poised. The emotions you feel in a situation like that are difficult to explain. You're stressed out of your mind. You know an entire city, an entire fan base, is watching you. You know all your friends back home in Boston are watching your every move. You know the whole damn hockey world is watching you. It's scary and exhilarating all at the same time. On a warm Saturday night in Minnesota, I was feeling all those emotions when the puck dropped. I remember thinking to myself, *Remember your job. Trust yourself. Control your emotions. Respect your opponent. And win the fucking game.*

Julie and all the wives and girlfriends took a flight that day, so they were there with us. And we knew everyone back home—and when I say home, I'm talking about Pittsburgh—was behind us. We could feel it. And my God, were we ready.

Less than 10 seconds into the game, the North Stars took a penalty for charging into Tommy. Dumb move. We could smell their desperation. At the end of the power play, Ulfie flicked one past Casey from the left point, and we were off and running. Mario took a great pass from Murph and made it 2–0 later in the first, and then Joey Mullen made it 3–0.

But we were calm in the locker room. No one was celebrating. Not even close. We stayed poised, just the way Badger Bob wanted.

We really blew the game open in the second period. Bob Errey scored to make it 4–0, then Ronnie and Joey scored on breakaways. Just like that, it was 6–0 through two.

Also in the second period, Mark Recchi got hurt by a cheap shot from Jimmy Johnson, our old teammate. Jimmy is a great guy, but it was a dirty hit. And boy did we let him hear it. Rex kept calling him a "fucking backstabber" from the bench. Rex was really banged up and didn't play the rest of the night. It was a horrible hit from behind. It could have broken his neck. Jesus, did we let him have it. Here's a sample of some things we said from the bench to Jimmy: "Thank God we traded you, you fucking fuck."

I think that about covered it. I feel bad about it now because, like I said, he was a great guy. But these are the things that are said in the heat of battle, and we were all pretty upset about the hit that Rex took.

In the third period, Jimmy Paek and Murph scored to make it 8–0. Believe it or not, though, I still didn't feel comfortable. I was so intensely into the game. We had blown big leads before and, even though I don't think a team in hockey history has ever blown an 8–0 lead, I swear to God, I was still nervous. That was just my mentality. I wasn't taking anything for granted on that night.

Finally, with two minutes left in the third period, I could finally relax. I took a deep breath. All that anxiety was finally gone. And I looked at Rex. "Hey Rex," I said. "We're gonna win the Cup."

He looked over at me and smiled. "Fucking right, Bubs."

Finally, we could just enjoy it. We had absolutely ambushed them on their home ice, a place where they almost never lost that spring. There would be no parade for them. We were never going to lose that series. Finally, we had put it all together and we were champions. As the seconds ticked down, I just remember the pure joy that I felt. There's nothing like it.

We all stormed around Tommy when it was over. People used to say he couldn't win the big game, but that most certainly wasn't true, and he proved it over and over again that spring. It was such a surreal, joyous feeling. Mario won the Conn Smythe, as if there was ever a doubt. Artie scored 17 goals that playoff year; Rex was amazing, and Tommy was worthy, too. But Mario was the guy. He was our leader and he put up 44 points in 23 games during the playoffs. Let that number register for a minute.

Finally, they brought the Cup onto the ice. Nowadays, it's very orderly. The captain takes the Cup and skates with it, then the veterans line up, one by one, and take their turn. We did things a little differently and, honestly, I prefer the way we did it. It was a free-for-all. We all skated up to Mario when he raised the Cup and surrounded him. We all wanted to touch that Cup. It was just a totally organic thing. You know what it was? It was perfect.

What an honor it was to have Bryan Trottier hand me the Cup. Of all people, to have one of the great players in hockey history, a special leader if there's ever been one, hand you the Cup? Damn. It still leaves me speechless, to be quite honest.

The party was just beginning.

One by one, the Cup was passed. It was funny how each guy instinctively knew who to hand the Cup to. It's a funny thing how that works. Everything about the celebration was incredible. You feel like you're on top of the world. There's not another feeling in the world like it.

We went back to the locker room, and you couldn't even move in there. I don't know who all the people were there. Julie was there, as were lots of wives and girlfriends. There were lots of family members, lots of media. It was a wild scene, but none of us even thought about complaining. We were strictly in the moment and having the time of our lives. I remember leaving the locker room at one point to do an interview. At that point, I had kind of a spiritual moment. Listen, I won't lie. I wasn't the most God-fearing person in the world. I believed what I believed, but I wasn't what you would consider religious by any stretch. But at that moment, I started thinking back to earlier in the day, when I found that church. I'm so glad I started that little personal tradition and I hope I get many more opportunities to find churches on the day when the Penguins have a chance to win the Stanley Cup.

(It's not always easy, by the way. I had to rent a car in San Jose in 2016 and go find one, but all's well that ends well. The church I found was about to be closed, but a lady was working there. She told me she usually wasn't there at that time, but that she'd let me in. I told her I had something very important to pray about. She told me to take my time. I was raised Catholic, so I went in there and prayed as hard as I could for the Pittsburgh Penguins. I lit a candle and everything.)

The party in the locker room was sensational, but we were just getting started. As much fun as we were having, we needed to get home to Pittsburgh so the real party could begin. And boy, that flight home was the best flight of my life. Minneapolis to Pittsburgh is about a two-hour flight. By the time we got on the plane, let's just say, we were all feeling good. Halfway through the flight, the captain came on the loud speaker and said something I'll never forgot. "Congratulations, boys. Also, we wanted to let you know, there are 10,000 fans waiting for you at Pittsburgh International Airport."

We all erupted when we heard that. I think that made us about as happy as anything that night. Seriously. It made us all feel like a million bucks to know so many fans were waiting for us. About 10 minutes later, however, the captain came back on the loudspeaker.

"An update from Pittsburgh International: there are 20,000 fans waiting for you."

The plane went crazy. A few minutes later, he came on the loudspeaker again.

"An update from Pittsburgh International: we are now told that 30,000 fans are waiting in the terminal for you guys."

At this point, we didn't know what to believe. We're all drunk and not really sure if this captain is fucking around with us or not. We were hoping it was real, but we didn't know what to think at that point in time. And wouldn't you know it, the pilot decided to give us one more update.

"An update from Pittsburgh International: you won't believe this, but we're now being told that 40,000 fans are waiting for you in the terminal."

We let out the biggest roar, hoping it was true. And was it ever. When we got to our gate at Pittsburgh International, it was like nothing we had ever seen. That was before the days of 9/11. Anybody could walk into the airport if they pleased. Also, it was the perfect storm of events: it was a Saturday night on Memorial Day Weekend, the weather was perfect, and the city was absolutely in love with us. Put it all together, and that's how you get 40,000 fans at the airport when we arrived at 4:00 AM.

Don't get me wrong, it was one of the most amazing moments of my life, seeing all of those fans. But it was also pretty scary. Truth be told, I feared for my life that night. Seeing that many people, without much in the way of law and order, I was totally uncomfortable. Holy shit. Remember, I'm prone to anxiety. And I'd literally never seen so many people in my life. It was total chaos. There's footage out there on YouTube from that night. You can see the look of fear on my face, walking through the crowd. I was loving it and terrified all at the same time. We wouldn't have changed anything about that evening, but a lot of people on the team were rattled by how many people there were, how loud it was, and how emotionally

Mario and the Cup: a perfect match. (AP Images)

charged the whole atmosphere was. It had been 12 years since the city of Pittsburgh tasted a championship and all that frustration was released on that night.

This is where things got really fucked up. We got to the school buses that were waiting for us in the parking lot. That's right; yellow school buses. And we were sitting there forever because it was total gridlock. There's no air conditioning on those buses. Holy shit was it hot that night, too. I always remember how hot out it was that night for a May evening. I've never seen people sweating so much in my life. Bob Errey's wife, Tracy, started hyperventilating. It was insane.

The school buses couldn't get us to our cars because of all the people. We literally couldn't get there and, honestly, we shouldn't have been driving anyway, so it was a blessing. They were able to get us out of the parking lot, so the buses took us to Tommy Barrasso's house in Sewickley.

How's this for a visual? It's 6:00 AM, the sun is starting to rise, the Stanley Cup is sitting in the front yard at Tommy's house, and there are people partying everywhere. And you know what? I just wanted to go home. It was all too much. You always hear about people going days without sleeping after winning the Cup because they're partying so much. That's total bullshit. You sleep. Trust me, everyone sleeps at some point, and at that point in time, all I wanted to do was sleep. Julie and I wanted to get home to our house in Upper St. Clair. The school bus drivers said they would take us to our respective homes.

We were at the Business 60 interchange right off the parkway just trying to get past the old airport and to my house. And what happens? The fucking bus runs out of gas. Seriously. I'm having the best night of my life, but at this point, I'm feeling a little impatient. The sun is up. We get out of the bus. I just wanted to get home and sleep. It's all I could think about. I didn't know what else to do, so

I threw my thumb in the air and started to hitchhike. Pittsburgh is the kind of town where you just trust people, you know? So, Julie and I just started to hitchhike. Suddenly, some guy slams on the brakes and snaps his neck back to look at us. He pulls up and says, "Hey, are you Phil Bourque? What are you doing?"

I said, "Yeah, I'm Phil Bourque. I just won the Cup, and I want to go home."

The guy says, "Well, I'm on my way to work. But fuck it. I'm driving you home."

And so the guy took me and Julie home. I wasn't the only one to hitchhike that night, by the way. Jimmy Paek did it. Grant Jennings, too. A couple of others. It's not normally the kind of thing a right-thinking person would do, and I don't think I've ever hitchhiked in my life other than that moment. But there's just something different about Pittsburgh, about Penguins fans, about all the sports fans in this town. At that point in time, I wasn't the least bit nervous or worried about anything. Even though we were all drunk and barely knew what we were doing, we knew that, somehow, some way, the good people of Pittsburgh were going to get me and my wife home safely.

You have no idea how happy I was to get home and sleep in my bed, knowing I was a Stanley Cup champion, knowing 40,000 Pittsburghers showed up at the airport to greet us. It was the greatest night of my life. It was the greatest night of all our lives.

And let me tell you, I slept for more than two hours in a row on that night. No sleeping pills necessary.

CHAPTER 11
THE BEST AND WORST SUMMER

The Stanley Cup party went on for a few days. It peaked on May 28 when we had a parade in downtown Pittsburgh. We gathered at Point State Park at noon on a Tuesday, and nearly 100,000 people showed up. It was a carnival of black and gold. We were all a little hungover, but trust me, we put aside those headaches and had the time of our lives. I gave a speech that some of you may remember, as I proclaimed, "What do you say we take this out on the river and party all summer?" Yeah, that was me in a nutshell. I was truly having the time of my life.

Later in the summer was my time to have the Stanley Cup and, while I was from Boston, I planned on having the Cup at my home in Upper St. Clair. I was a Pittsburgher by this point. Guys only get the Cup for a day these days, but back then, it was a little different. We all got the Cup for two days, which was really great. I was quite excited about my time with the Cup. And then, the news got even sweeter.

It was a Friday afternoon and I was just hanging out at home. Suddenly, my phone rings. It was Paul Martha, the Penguins president.

"Hey Bourquey," he started. "Listen, I'm supposed to have the Cup all weekend, for the next three days. But something came up. I've got to get out of town. I'm at the arena now, and I just happened to look at the Cup schedule. I see you're supposed to have the Cup on Monday and Tuesday next week. So, I was thinking, how about you just take the Cup for my three days and then you can still have it for your two days? So you can just have it for five straight days. I'll figure out another time for me to have the Cup. No big deal. But here's the thing, Bourquey. I've got to get to the airport really soon, so I need you to get down to the arena right now, so you can get the Cup. Does that work?"

Does that fucking work? I broke so many traffic laws on my way to pick up the Cup. I was driving on curbs. I was driving through

HOV lanes. I was blowing through every red light. I drove like a complete asshole on Rt. 19 all the way into Pittsburgh, and I got there in time to secure the Cup. And keep in mind, this was before Phil Pritchard, the keeper of the Cup, any of that stuff. It was just me and the Stanley Cup. For five days. Oh my God.

The first thing I did was call my friend who lived in Maryland, Tom Yovienne. He lived on the eastern shore in Maryland, and it's beautiful there in the summer. I told him I had a little surprise for him and that I was coming for a visit. I had the Cup on a Friday in Pittsburgh. I went to all the bars I used to frequent. I just walked right into the bars with the Cup, yelling, "Fucking right!" Some of them didn't have more than a few people, but whatever. Everyone there was going to be drinking out of the Cup as far as I was concerned, and that's exactly what happened. I did that for a little while before making my way to Maryland.

I had a big Ford Bronco at the time. It wasn't O.J.'s model, but it was a nice one. I threw the Cup in the back and was on my way to Easton, Maryland. On Friday night, I walked right down Main Street with the Stanley Cup in my hands. I told Tom to meet me at a bar down there and I surprised him with it. He couldn't believe it. We drank all night long—me, Tom, and the Cup. Of course, this was the weekend when I may have damaged the Stanley Cup just a little bit.

Yeah, that really happened. I made my way back to Pittsburgh afterward and I was just taking the Cup everywhere. You name it, I probably took the Cup there. I wanted everyone to experience it, to soak it in. I wanted the whole city to drink out of the Cup and trust me, I did my part.

On my last night with the Cup, I was just sitting there in my living room, looking at that beautiful trophy. I was reading all the names, checking it out, really appreciating the moment. I had to give it up the next day, so I wanted to enjoy every single second with it. Then I noticed something. The damn thing was damaged. It wasn't horrible, but the top of the Cup was totally out of place. Oh boy. I couldn't exactly return the Cup to the president of the Penguins looking like that. Something was loose. I'm not exactly a handy man, but I did have a red tool box under my kitchen sink. I thought about it for a few minutes, and then I went to work. I had the flashlight in my mouth, laying there on the floor, shining it into the Cup to figure out the problem. My whole head is inside of the Cup. It's just plastic covering. So I removed the plastic cover and looked inside. It was so hollow. Then I see this one nut had come loose from the original bolt. Thank God. It was something even I could fix easily. So I tightened it up and basically put the Stanley Cup back together properly. Trust me, I felt a lot better when I managed to take care of that.

Of course, I had some fun while I was pulling the thing apart to fix it. When I looked inside, I noticed that three French guys who had repaired it in the past had engraved their names on the inside of the Cup. I never knew anyone had done anything like that before. So the light bulb went off in my head at that very moment. I figured it wouldn't be such a bad idea if I signed my name, too. So, I left an inscription for someone in the future to read: ENJOY IT. PHIL BOURQUE, PITTSBURGH PENGUINS, '91 CHAMPS.

For quite some time, I was one of only four people to have my name on the outside and the inside of the Stanley Cup. In 2001, we had a 10-year Cup reunion. By that time, the Keepers of the Cup were a thing, probably because of people such as me. I introduced myself to Phil Pritchard. He smiled and said he knew who I was. Uh oh. So, I asked him if he knew about my name being on the inside of the Cup. "Oh," he said, "We know all about it." I asked him if I was in trouble. "God no," he said. "We loved it. It's still in there, but when the new band goes on the Cup, we have to take

It's pretty special to have been around this organization for all five of its Cup championships, two of my own. (AP Images)

one off, so it will probably be coming off." I told him, "Oh, that's perfectly fine. I just didn't want to be in trouble."

It was a wild summer. I was still training and things of that nature, but it was hard not to be a little distracted. I wanted everyone to party all summer, and that's pretty much what I did. Hell, I even got married in August. Julie and I finally tied the knot in Vegas, naturally.

Later in August, the perfect summer went straight to hell.

Not long after I was back in Pittsburgh, I was informed that Badger Bob was sick, that there was something wrong with his brain. The moment I heard about it, something came over me. It was so powerful. I literally heard a voice in my head, and it told me to go see Bob immediately. So that's what I did. I got on the phone with Craig Patrick and he told me that Bob was at Mercy

Hospital. I immediately drove into the city and made my way to his hospital room. There were nurses everywhere, and they told me I wasn't allowed to see him because I wasn't family. I looked at them and said, "That's my head coach. I'm going in his room." They finally let me in.

Bob looked absolutely terrible. He was hooked up to all these machines. If I didn't know any better, I would have barely recognized him. It didn't look like Bob at all. It was terrible. Luckily, he was still somewhat coherent even though I know he was on all kinds of medication at that point in time. He had endured an aneurysm and they found out he had brain cancer. We didn't know it at the time, but the prognosis was grave. Even though he was a little disoriented, he knew it was me. I didn't know what to do. I was just standing there staring at my head coach, this man I had grown to love so very much. He grabbed my hand. "Bourquey," he said. "I heard you got married. Congratulations to you both. And I'm happy for you. I think you need it. It will be good for you." Bob knew I partied too much. He was always worried about that and he wanted me to settle down a little bit. It meant so much to me that he cared as much as he did.

Here's the thing about Bob. He was the most optimistic person on Earth, and that optimism inspired optimism from other people. I knew he was in trouble. The writing was on the wall. Bob looked awful, and he was in rough shape. But as I walked out of the hospital room that day, I thought to myself, "It's Badger Bob. He's going to be just fine. He'll be behind the bench when the season starts in October."

He was still too sick to be around during training camp. Again, this should have been a red flag, but we all kind of brushed it off. Some guys had heard that Bob wasn't doing well, but we kept believing he would be fine. They had moved him to a hospital in Colorado

Springs. As fate would have it, we played a neutral site exhibition game out there in September. The league was trying to grow hockey's popularity, so we had exhibition games in places like Colorado, San Francisco, and Texas. We were excited because we were told that Bob would be coming to our game to see us play. Perfect. We were fired up for that, of course.

I never looked in the crowd during games. Never. It made me too nervous. But when we were told Bob was in the crowd, we all looked up. And I'm glad he showed up, of course. But it wasn't a pretty picture. About 20 rows up, at the back of the main concourse, was Bob. However, he was in a hospital bed. Literally. He came straight from the hospital to the rink in a hospital bed. I would guess that Bob probably knew he was getting close to the end, and I think he just wanted to see us play. He gave us so much joy as our head coach and I think we gave him a lot of joy, too. So, even though he couldn't get out of bed, he came to a cold rink just to watch us skate. Think about that. That's the kind of man he was.

Even after we left him, I still thought he was going to be okay. Crazy, I know. I was brainwashing myself. In reality, deep down, that trip kind of told us that Bob wasn't ever coaching again, that Bob probably wasn't long for the world. We weren't stupid. We had to know. But I was brainwashing myself and I think a lot of my teammates were doing the same thing. We would say things like, "Well, maybe Bob won't be back until Thanksgiving, but of course he's going to be back at some point this season. So what if he's not ready for the start of the season? Bob needs to take his time and, when he's ready, he'll be back behind the bench with that same smile on his face."

When we got home, we had a special ceremony to receive our Stanley Cup rings at the Igloo Club. The way it was set up was beautiful. There was a camera in the club and a big satellite truck. We were able to beam the ceremony live to Bob's hospital room so that he could be a part of it. Every single one of us got in front of the camera and gave him a nice message. We were all so positive, just like he would have been.

"We love you, Bob. We know we'll be seeing you soon."

"We know this is just a hiccup, Badger. We'll see you in no time."

It was a special moment, but it was sad, too. The reality of his condition was settling in, even if we tried to believe otherwise.

It was hard to believe that a human being who was so incredibly full of life could be so close to death. Quite frankly, a part of me still refused to believe it. Bob was the guy who taught us so much more about life than he did about hockey. His famous slogan was, "It's a great day for hockey." And while it's a great slogan, the truth is, Bob was about so much more than hockey. He was basically like a life coach and a hockey coach all in one beautiful package. Bob cared more about me settling down and being a good husband and a good guy than he cared about how many goals I could score or how many penalties I could kill. Seriously. He was that guy, the ultimate human being.

Scotty Bowman was named the interim head coach while Bob was away from the team. How's that for a replacement? We always respected Scotty, obviously. And you know what? He's actually a really good guy. He didn't have the greatest personality in the world and could be cold, but he wasn't a bad guy. The thing was, though, he wasn't Bob. No one was.

We started out the season in pretty good form. We knew we didn't have to be at our best in the regular season, and we weren't. But we also knew Bob was probably watching, and we wanted to be playing at our very best for him. Still, something just wasn't right. Good coaches always command a certain amount of respect and form a certain bond with a team. That's normal. What we had with

Bob was something greater. We had gone through so many coaches in Pittsburgh since the early '80s. It's pretty common in the NHL to go through coaches, but honestly, we had developed a bit of a reputation for being a coach-killing team. I don't think it's entirely fair, but we weren't the easiest team to coach—put it that way. In Bob, we had finally found our guy. It was magic. We'd have done anything for that man. As October turned into November and the season got into full swing, we realized that one special season with Bob was all we were ever going to have.

CHAPTER 12
ONE FOR
THE BADGER

As fate would have it, Bob never made it back behind our bench. He never even made it back to Pittsburgh. He died right before Thanksgiving. You'd think I'd remember all the details of when he died, like exactly where I was and who told me. Stuff like that. But I don't. I was so devastated that I have almost literally blacked all of it out of my mind, out of my memory. All I remember is that I felt a sense of grief that was way, way too powerful for me to properly process.

But I remember what happened a couple of nights later. We had a home game at the Igloo and we held a candlelight vigil before the game. If you were there that night, you remember it. Every person in the crowd had a candle and all the Penguins, myself included, stood in a circle at center ice. We won that night and I have no idea how. We could barely function. But we beat the Devils 8–4. I had a goal and two assists that night, and I don't have a clue how I pulled that off. During the pregame ceremony, we were all crying. Every damn one of us—even the guys who weren't really emotional by nature. I can still hear the noises of grown men sobbing. It was the most awful thing I've ever felt in my life, that pain of knowing that Bob was gone, that only his memory remained. Before the game, I just totally lost it. It was the end of a very beautiful chapter for all of us.

The team chartered a plane and we took a flight to Colorado for the funeral. That whole day is such a blur to me. But I do remember how many of his former players were there. Guys he coached in college, guys he coached with the Flames, executives and coaches from around the league...they were all there to pay their respects to Bob. That's how beloved he was. Everyone shut down what they were doing and paid homage to this incredible man.

It got me thinking about Bob's legacy. Go through all the major sports and answer me this question: What coach had more impact than Bob in one single season? Seriously, can you name one? We speak of him as though he were around the Penguins for 15 years. His slogan, "It's a great day for hockey," is still on the ice when the Penguins play home games. It wasn't 15 years, though. It was one fucking year. One. That's it. And yet the very fiber of the organization all goes back to Bob, his sayings, his slogans, his beliefs, his positive energy, his love for the game, his love for the Pittsburgh Penguins. It blows me away when I think about that man's legacy.

And you know what's really amazing? Mario only played a grand total of 49 games for Bob, and that's including the playoffs. Only 49. The greatest Penguin of them all and the greatest Penguins coach of them all only worked together 49 times. Of course, we went 31–15–3 in those games against the toughest of competition, which is probably no shock. What a combination those two were. You know, I never saw Mario react to a coach like he reacted to Badger. Mario had a ton of coaches in his career. He wasn't a coach killer, but there were some coaches he didn't care for. It's human nature, especially when you're a superstar. But Bob won him over immediately. It had nothing to do with Xs and Os, even though Bob was the perfect coach for Mario. See, Mario was a natural. The ultimate natural. He didn't need a coach telling him how to play hockey. But what Mario loved about Bob was the person he was. He just had a way of keeping Mario happy at all times, even when his back was driving him crazy. Mario just loved him so damn much. I can still picture just the way Mario would smile at the guy. Even when he was hurting or out of the lineup, Mario wanted to be around Bob. That was a big deal for us. You always want your leader, your superstar, to be happy. Mario loved Bob just as much as the rest of us did.

We still had a season to play and we were now on a mission to win a championship in Bob's memory. We didn't really talk about it a ton, but we did on occasion. We knew what we had to do, though. We knew.

Scotty was the man in charge. Talk about oil and water. Bob was so warm, so lovable. Scotty was Scotty. We didn't hate Scotty, though. I want to make that clear. You always hear the story about all of us telling Scotty we didn't want him around at practices. It's true, we didn't love how he ran practices. He was just so different than Bob, and it was a terrible adjustment for us. But there was way more to the story. We found out Scotty had a sick child back in Buffalo. When we learned about that, we told him just to stay there unless we had a game to play. Sure, we didn't really love having him around. But we really didn't need him at practices and taking care of his kid was way more important. We basically just wanted Barry Smith and Rick Kehoe to run practices and we wanted Scotty to do what Scotty did best. In the history of the game, there's never been a better bench coach than Scotty. Total, total genius. It was unreal. He had this memory for the game that was like nothing I've seen before or since. He knew all our strengths and weaknesses. He also knew all our opponents' strengths and weakness. The man was a walking encyclopedia. Scotty was literally a fucking genius. But he didn't really have a great personality for us. Bob would laugh at our jokes, and while he probably didn't approve of some of our off-ice behavior, he never judged. He had a way of seeing the best in people. Scotty was just a tough nut to crack. You knew he was smarter than you and he could rub you the wrong way, quite honestly. But we also realized that he was in an impossible position. He truly was. We weren't going to be thrilled with any coach after Bob passed. It simply wasn't possible. So, if you're going to replace with him anyone, it might as well be the greatest hockey tactician who ever lived.

We didn't have much of a regular season. Mario won the scoring title but still missed 20 games with back issues. More than anything, we had a hangover. That was it. That was the problem. Consider everything that was going on. We won the Cup for the first time. We partied like a bunch of idiots. Did we party too much that summer? Yes, we did. We were a bunch of drunken sailors that whole summer. It was totally out of control, and when you party too much, you start to lose your edge. Then Bob got sick. Then Bob died. Scotty takes over. We're a little full of ourselves as a hockey team. That's a lot of shit going on all at the same time. As a result, we were never in any danger of missing the playoffs, but we were never in any real danger of beating out the Rangers or the Capitals for the Patrick Division title.

Through January and February, we were fucking rotten. In fact, we had a 25-game stretch that saw us go 6–15–4. Really. A team with all that talent, and with Scotty Bowman behind the bench, actually went 6–15–4 during that stretch. It was embarrassing.

On March 3, everything changed. To me, it was one of the most important days in franchise history. Here's why.

We were in Calgary at a downtown hotel. We played the Flames the next night. Craig Patrick called the entire team into a ballroom for a meeting. No Scotty. Just Craig and the players. That was it. At that time, we were so bad that we were actually flirting with missing the playoffs. It was bad. Really bad. Craig pulled a bunch of tables to the middle of the room so we were all sitting close together. And then he started talking.

"I'm not happy with the way things are going," he said. "So, if you have something to say, now is your opportunity. Please. Raise your hand. Stand up. Say what's in your heart and what's on your mind. I want to hear what all of you have to say. I want to know what's wrong."

One by one, we stood. I can still remember Trots talking. Peter Taglianetti. Troy Loney. Guys got up and voiced their frustrations. It was a hell of a thing to see.

And you'll never believe what I did. I stood up. And I said, "Craig, it's pretty simple. I think there is a disconnect between Scotty and us. I really believe that. I know you don't want to hear this, but I don't think we can win the Stanley Cup with Scotty Bowman as our head coach."

Then I sat down. The whole room turned silent seconds after I said that we couldn't win with the greatest coach of all time as our general. It was a ballsy thing to say, I guess. And hell, I was a free agent that summer, so Craig very easily could have traded me that day if he wanted to, I'm sure. He knew I wasn't a bad apple, though. I was talking from the heart. I just didn't give a shit anymore. I was so damn hungry to win and so upset with how we were playing, I was going to say something about it.

For all of Craig's amazing attributes, the thing he does best is listen. He didn't say anything immediately when he heard me speak. He sat there, and he listened. He listened to all of us, man to man. You could see him taking it all in, listening to what we had to say. It was evident that he had total respect for us as hockey players and as people.

After taking it all in, Craig spoke. And he was quite to the point.

"I want to thank all of you for speaking up the way you did," Craig started. "I really appreciate it. I appreciate the way you guys all spoke your mind. I agree with what a lot of you said. But some things, I don't agree with. We're going to find a way. I'll tell you that. We're going to find a way to win with you guys and Scotty. You both need to meet in the middle a little bit. He's got to give some, and you guys have got to give some."

Then, Craig pointed right at me.

"I didn't agree with what you said, Bourquey," Craig said. "I know we can all win together, you guys and Scotty. And we're going to win the Stanley Cup."

Then, he walked out of the room.

That was a crossroads moment for our team. And holy shit did we heat up at that point. Along the way, of course, Craig made another blockbuster deal. The year before, it had been Ronnie and Ulfie who made such an enormous difference.

This time around, Craig and Scotty agreed we needed to get tougher. Craig went out and got us Rick Tocchet, Ken Wregget, and Kjell Samuelsson from the Flyers. Holy shit. Of course, in return, we dealt away two Hall of Famers in Paul Coffey and Mark Recchi. Talk about a blockbuster.

I do believe Scotty had a lot of influence on that trade. I don't think he was in love with Coff's game at that point. He was never huge on offensive-minded defensemen. I don't think he trusted them completely and, even though he would later coach Coff in Detroit, I do believe Scotty viewed him as a bit of a liability at that point in his career. I don't think Craig ever wanted to trade Rex, but he was going to be a free agent that summer and money was becoming an issue with the Penguins. There was some friction there with his contract. He was a star and wanted to be paid like one.

Losing Rex was hard for me on a personal level. Really hard. We lived together during the 1989–90 season. Of all my teammates in my years of playing professional hockey, I'd label Rex as my favorite teammate ever. On and off the ice, this guy was special. Sometimes we'd be on the same line together and we always had instant chemistry. We had the same chemistry off the ice, too. There was just something magical about him. I love the guy to death. And here's all you need to know about Rex.

The Flyers were really bad that year and didn't make the playoffs. When their season was over, Rex still lived in Pittsburgh. So, what did he do? He attended every damn one of our playoff games and sat with our family and friends. He was there every night. We'd see him after games and give him a hug. I doubt the Flyers would want to know that, but Rex was still there pulling for us. I'm sure, in a way, it hurt like hell for him. He's playing on this shitty team now and I think, deep down, we knew we were going to win it all again. I bet he knew it too, and I'm sure that was so hard. But there he was at Civic Arena, taking in every playoff game and pulling for us on and off the ice. It was strange for us because, while we immediately fell in love with Dicky Tocchet, we felt like Rex was always supposed to be a member of the Penguins. He meant that much to us. I always gave him so much credit, though. And he was a part of that team even though he was traded. He was one of the guys who got us there. I'll tell you the same thing about Johnny Cullen the year before. We don't even make the playoffs in 1991 without Johnny's contributions and, when we won the Cup that year, he was the first person I thought about. Just because a guy gets traded doesn't mean he wasn't part of what made your team special that season.

Of course, the 1992 playoffs almost didn't happen. There was a work stoppage that lasted about 10 days. Alan Eagleson represented the NHLPA and let me tell you—none of us trusted that guy for a fucking second. There was some shady shit going on. We were totally a slave to the PA at that point in time. We were so uninformed. We had no clue how much money other players in the league were making. We knew nothing about the finances of the game. That was the first time I realized that the NHL truly is a business, that it's not just about the game. It was a strange time.

Luckily, the playoffs happened, even if they were 10 days late. Someone forgot to tell us about the playoffs starting, though. We got shit kicked in Washington in each of the first two games of the series. We came back to win Game 3, but then we were truly embarrassed in Game 4 at home. Dino Ciccarelli, who we didn't particularly care for, scored four fucking goals in Game 4 and we lost 7–2. That was the only time in my career that I remember getting booed off the ice in Pittsburgh. We weren't upset that the fans treated us like that, either. They were so angry—and they had every right to be. We embarrassed ourselves that night. Something was wrong and, as a result, we were one game away from elimination. Keep in mind, the Capitals had the second-best record in hockey that season and the NHL's best collection of defensemen. You could say we were in trouble. Then again, I never thought we were dead. Not for one second.

On the morning of Game 5, I was sitting in the locker room in Landover, Maryland. There was a little walkway that went back toward the coach's offices there. I saw Mario, Trots, Ronnie, and Murph walking back after the morning skate. They held a big meeting. They wanted to be proactive. Everyone did. We were all so pissed off at ourselves. No one really thought we were going to lose the series. No one. But we knew something was wrong.

So, the leaders of our team decided to change our system on the fly. We were going to a 1-4. Basically, we were going to trap the shit out of them, which is kind of funny. We hated the trap, hated defensive-minded, conservative hockey. We were all about speed and talent. But we decided, as a team, to make the switch. I remember thinking to myself, *Fucking right. We've got nothing to lose.*

We knew it might work, that it could surprise them. It turned out to be brilliant. The Caps had all these defensemen who loved to jump into the play. So, guess what? We were sitting back and waiting for it, and we just forced them into one turnover after another. All we did was counter-attack the hell out of them. We won Game 5. Then Mario had a six-point game back at home, and we won Game 6 by a 6–4 final. They were rattled, and we could sense it. Suddenly, Tommy was playing better. Mario was totally locked in. Jagr was making the Capitals look stupid. It was all coming together. Still, we had to stroll into Washington and find a way to win Game 7.

It was no problem even though it was a close game. Mario and Jagr scored. Joey Mullen added an empty-netter and we held on to win it 3–1. Mario put up 17 points in the final five games of the series so, obviously, he led the way. He was probably at the height of his power at that point in time. But we didn't win that series just because of him. There were stars everywhere on our roster, and they all turned it up a notch. Every damn one of them. And the trapping worked. It totally screwed with the Capitals, and they never really recovered. It taught us that, if we played defense, we were almost impossible to beat because we were always going to score goals no matter what.

Now, I've got to tell you, I played 18 years of hockey professionally. I won the Cup twice. I won a lot of huge games, a lot of series. But I never celebrated more than in Game 7 in Washington. Joey put the game away with an empty-netter. Back then, there was a tiny little sliver of glass that separated the benches. I happened to be at the very end of the bench, right beside Washington's bench. I leaned over the glass and yelled at them, "Fuck you! Fuck you! Fuck you! Fuck all of you fucking fucks!" I never celebrated another win in my life like I did that one. The emotion I felt was indescribable. They had us by the throat. We hated Dino and Dale Hunter. They were always running their fucking mouths. We still had Badger Bob on our minds. Everyone thought we were done, that we were a one-hit wonder. That motivated us so much. So, all that emotion came out of me when we found a way to win that series. Yeah, we had a lot of talent. Everyone knows that. But it was the guts that we showed in that series that told me so much about the people in that locker room.

Next up were the Rangers, the best team in the regular season. Christ, did we hate them.

We won Game 1 at the Garden convincingly. We were really rolling. Then along came Adam Graves, who broke Mario's hand with a slash, knocking the big guy out of the series. So, did Graves do it with the intention of hurting Mario? It's funny; I would later play for the Rangers, so eventually I got a different perspective. Roger Neilson was their coach. My read on the situation, in retrospect, was that Neilson encouraged players on his roster—especially certain guys, like Graves and Kris King—to go after Mario. I believe that. That was the impression I was under, that he wanted them to take Mario out. Maybe it wasn't supposed to be a slash on the hand specifically. I really don't know. But I think they wanted to take him out, that they realized they couldn't beat us with the big guy in the lineup. Mario was unstoppable at that time, and they knew it.

They came back and beat us in Game 2. We were in shock. Then King scored in overtime and they won Game 3. Making matters worse, the fucking league didn't suspend Graves until just before Game 4. Why, I'll never know. We were so angry. There had been so much hostility between these two teams and they were always taking runs at Mario. David Shaw knocked him out cold with a slash to the throat on October 30, 1988. We wouldn't let Shaw off the ice.

In Game 3, in fact, I did the one thing in my career that I regret.

I can still hear Scotty before the game. "Nobody touches him. Not one person. Don't worry about him. We're here to win the game."

I was kind of pissed. We all wanted blood. We wanted Graves to pay for what he did. But at the same time, I wanted to listen to my coach. So, during Game 3, I got Graves alone in the corner. I looked up and saw that the ref—and remember, there was only one ref at that time—was on the opposite end of the rink. So, I hocked up the biggest loogie of my life, and I spit right in his face. He didn't even do anything. He yelled "Fuck you" at me but then just skated back to the bench. I think he knew he was going to have to pay. I do regret that. I shouldn't have done it, and Scotty would have been very upset with me had he seen it. I don't think anyone saw it, to be honest. Maybe the people in the front row, but that's about it. Still, I hated that son of a bitch at that time and wanted him to be humiliated. The fact that they let him play that night when he intentionally took Mario out still angers us.

The rest of the series saw us do some special things. We were down 4–2 in the third period of Game 4, but then Ronnie beat Mike Richter from the blue line. Troy Loney tied it. Then Ronnie capped off the hat trick in overtime in maybe the best game of his life.

In Game 5, Jagr went to another stratosphere. Jesus. He made all their defensemen look so stupid. He scored on a penalty shot, then won the game in the third period with a ridiculous goal. It was one of the great performances of his career. The kid was so clutch.

Game 6 was an ass-kicking. We had taken their hearts. They were done. We pounded the shit out of them 5–1. When it was over, our fans kept chanting "nineteen-forty" over and over again, letting the Rags remember the most recent time they had won the Cup.

For the conference final, it was back to my hometown once again. And it really wasn't a series. Mario and Ray Bourque missed Game 1 with injuries, but Jagr again came through in the clutch, winning it in overtime. Mario came back in Game 2, and the Bruins might as well have just forfeited. The atmosphere when he came back was electric. He scored two goals in his first game back and we just put on a show the rest of the series. We destroyed them in a sweep. Mario scored his famous goal where he put the puck between Bourque's legs and then beat Andy Moog top shelf. Artie was unreal that series. He had a four-goal game. We were at the very

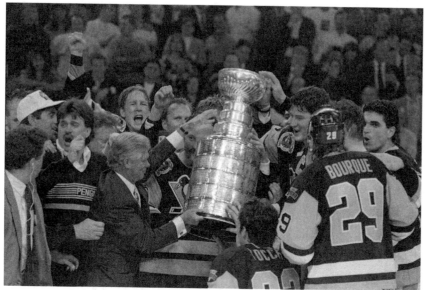

There's no better feeling than this. (AP Images)

height of our power, the talent and character all shining through at once. We literally made the Bruins look like a mite team. We really did. And that was a good Boston team. They were a legitimate Cup contender. But we made them look stupid the entire series. It was an incredible display.

Speaking of incredible, the Blackhawks had won 11 straight games going into the Final. We had won seven straight. Are you kidding me? It doesn't get much better.

Boy did they silence the Igloo in Game 1. Before we knew it, we were down 3–0. I couldn't believe it.

We had a power play late in the first period, and nothing was cooking. Someone came to the bench, and I had my Gilly moment. I said, "Fuck it," and jumped onto the ice because no one else did. Then, Bobby Errey gave me a hell of an assist.

It's funny, the things you talk about on the bench. Just a minute earlier, Bobby and I were sitting on the bench trying to break down Eddie Belfour. We felt like he was awkward when the puck was behind the net.

So, there I am on the power play, for some reason. I see the puck behind the net and I get there first. Then, I circle around and, suddenly, I could hear Bobby's voice in my head. I wanted to go for a wraparound, but then I figured it was best to stay patient. That's exactly what I did. I fired a shot at Belfour and it snuck through him.

Still, we fell behind 4–1, and it looked like we were screwed. But then Tocchet deflected a Paul Stanton shot past Belfour. Then Mario scored on his legendary bank shot, where he launched a puck off Belfour's ass and in. Of course he did it on purpose. It was never an accident with Mario.

Jagr then tied the game with perhaps his most famous goal, weaving through the Blackhawks before beating Belfour.

At that point, we were cool. Worst case, the game was going to overtime. We were comfortable with that because we knew we really didn't deserve to even be in the game. Then Mario drew a penalty and, a moment later, the Blackhawks left him all alone off an offensive zone draw. Great idea. Ronnie won the draw, Murph made an incredible play to get the puck through, and there was Mario to bury the rebound. It was the greatest goal in history, and I promise you it was the loudest that building has ever been. Civic Arena. Mellon Arena. Consol Energy Center. PPG Paints Arena. Whatever building, in whatever era, it's never been that loud. Not even close. It was an honor to be in the building that night. The place was literally shaking. It was the perfect storm. Best player in the world, amazing comeback, Stanley Cup Final, playing at home. Hell yes.

We ended up sweeping the Hawks, of course. The amazing thing was, all the games were so close. 5–4. 3–1. 1–0. 6–5.

It would have been tough for any coach to step in after Badger Bob died, but Scotty Bowman did it and led us to a Cup. (Getty Images)

It wasn't your conventional sweep. In that last game, they made the biggest mistake of all. They tried to play pond hockey with us. Big fucking mistake. I was playing on a line with Ronnie and Shawn McEachren that series, and I was on the ice when Ronnie buried the game winner on a two on one. We were in our element when we could skate. There was no team in the world—or maybe ever—that was keeping up with us in that kind of game. We knew Chicago had a great team, but we weren't afraid of anything. Not how tough they were, not how hot they were, not Chicago Stadium. We lived on the edge, man. There was nothing we loved more than that kind of challenge.

The locker room there felt like a sauna. It was so hot, so miserable. I felt like I couldn't breathe. But trust me, I had a smile on my face. You never forget your first one. In many ways, that night in Minnesota will always stand alone. Yet there was something even more satisfying about what we did in the 1992 Final. That was a harder road. We had a lot of injured players. The teams we had to face were way, way more daunting that season—the two best teams in the league, the Bruins and then the Blackhawks. And we won 11 straight. Come on. Who else could have pulled that off?

And the best thing of all? We did it for the Badger. I know he was up above looking down on us, and I know he was smiling at what we pulled off that spring. People can talk all they want about future Penguins teams or the 1992–93 squad. Bullshit. The 1992 Penguins were the greatest team in franchise history and proved it that spring.

CHAPTER 13
SAYING HELLO
TO THE ENEMY

The victory celebration was just as sweet the second time around. We held a championship rally at Three Rivers Stadium and, even though it was pouring down rain, the place was packed. There were some memorable moments. Trots took the Cup and went for a slide on the soaked tarp at the stadium, an indelible memory for anyone who was there. He was in many ways our most fearless leader but also our biggest kid. I made a rather memorable speech—okay, it was a poem—where I suggested to Mr. DeBartolo that perhaps Mario deserved a raise. (He got a big one a few months later.) The moment I most remember from that day, though, was the speech Scotty gave. Maybe he wasn't the warmest person in the world, but say this for Scotty: he knew we were Badger's team and he never lost focus of that. He handled everything in a very respectful way.

It's funny that I chose to mention Mario's contract. We all knew he was underpaid, but I was about to not be paid at all. At least, not by the Penguins. I was an unrestricted free agent as of July 1, 1992, and I had some pretty serious leverage. I turned 30 that June, so I was still close to the prime years of my career. I had two Stanley Cup rings. I had scored 52 goals in the previous three seasons, and I did so even after missing 22 games with an injury during the 1991–92 campaign. I had also scored nine postseason goals in the two previous playoff runs. I could kill penalties, I was fast, I could play above-average defense, and I was still pretty good at running the point on the power play. So yeah, I absolutely knew I was about to make some money.

I truly wanted to stay with the Penguins. Honestly, I was never distracted during the '92 playoffs. Never did I think about my contract. It was on the back burner for me. Winning a Cup was what mattered. Mission accomplished. So now it was time to get paid.

I could never envision myself playing for another team, but I had numbers in mind: I wanted a four-year contract, and I wanted

$500,000 per season. Maybe that doesn't sound like a ton of money by today's standards, but back then, $2 million guaranteed for a guy who wasn't a star was a big deal. I told my agent, Steve Bartlett, exactly what I wanted. The Penguins were having serious financial difficulties even though they were selling out games at the time. Civic Arena wasn't a big revenue-producing building, quite frankly, and Penguins ownership at the time wasn't swimming in money. Plus, think about the stars on that team: Mario Lemieux, Jaromir Jagr, Kevin Stevens, Rick Tocchet, Ron Francis, Joe Mullen, Tom Barrasso, Ulfie Samuelsson, Larry Murphy. It sounds like a freaking Hall of Fame wing. Those guys had to come first, and I understood that. But I still wanted to be taken care of. So, I went to free agency knowing in the back of my mind that I would still like the Penguins to match any offer.

July 1 arrived. I was up early. I was a little nervous but a little excited, too. At exactly 9:00 AM, my phone rang. It was Mike fucking Milbury. I was shocked. Are you kidding me? The guy who called Badger the Professor of Goonism? He was no longer Boston's coach, but he was the Bruins' general manager at that time. I'll never forget what he said to me: "I just wanted to be the first GM to give you a call this morning. I want you to know that I want you to play for the Boston Bruins, your hometown team."

He knew I was from Boston and probably knew a little bit of my heart was still in Boston. I mean, I appreciated him calling, I guess. But I was so surprised by it, and I really didn't have a clue what to say. I wasn't even ready to make a choice. So I said, "I appreciate your call. But listen, I rode the buses in the minors for a long time. And I haven't even finished celebrating winning the Cup yet. I appreciate the call. But I need some more time to think about it."

Interestingly enough, the Bruins never even made me an offer, which was a little odd. I never seriously considered playing there. Some guys want to play in their hometowns, but Pittsburgh was my home at this point in time. Late that month, things started to heat up. It wasn't a big bonanza on July 1 the way it is now. It took teams longer to make up their minds. But finally, I got two substantial offers. The San Jose Sharks and the New York Rangers each offered me four-year deals at $400,000 per season. Those offers had my attention. But apparently they didn't have my agent's attention. Steve, for reasons I'll never know, stopped returning my calls. He wasn't getting me information. It was so strange. The fact that I called him and left him messages, and he didn't bother calling me back, really hurt me. It felt like I couldn't trust him anymore, like I was being betrayed. So what did I do? I fired him. I was starting to panic, and my agent wasn't even speaking with me. I felt like I had no choice.

I had someone else in mind. I had met an agent named Ron Salcer years earlier. He lived out in L.A. and he represented a lot of us. Johnny Cullen, Jimmy Johnson, Bob Errey, and a few other guys. Sometimes you get to know other agents, and I felt really comfortable with him. Hell, this guy was always impressing us. He was good friends with Tony Danza and always took us on the set of *Who's the Boss?* So, if you're wondering how Robbie Brown and Alyssa Milano started dating, wonder no more. That's where it happened. He seemed like a good guy, and all the players he represented had nice things to say. I got his number and asked him to be my agent. He agreed, and I couldn't have been happier.

Steve wasn't happy when I told him I wanted to go in a different direction. He wasn't happy and reminded me that he had worked hard on my behalf. He wasn't a bad guy, but those few weeks left a bad taste in my mouth. I sent him a check for $1,500 as kind of a thank-you for his work. But I had moved on.

I made it clear with my new agent: I wanted a four-year deal and I wanted $500,000 per season. He knew San Jose and the Rangers were in the mix.

Two weeks later, Salcer gave me a call.

"Bourquey," he said, "the Rangers are ready to make a deal."

I was at my family's cottage in New Hampshire when this was going on. I was impressed it was happening, impressed the Rangers would give me the deal I wanted. It wasn't perfect. The cost of living in New York is rough and, hell, that was our biggest rival. I spat in the face of one of their players a couple of months earlier. Still, money talks, and I was willing to sign there. But I wasn't quite ready to call Smith. I wasn't quite ready to pull that trigger. Because even then, even as I was trying to set my financial future, I was always going to be loyal to the Pittsburgh Penguins. Always. So, I had an order for my new agent.

"Before we do this," I said, "I need you to do something. Call Craig. See if he's willing to match it. I don't really want to leave."

Salcer called Craig. It wasn't a long conversation.

"Craig said he can't match it," Rob said. "He told me to tell you to take the deal."

Damn. I understood, but it was still painful. Craig wanted to keep that team together forever. I know for a fact he did. He never wanted us split apart. But the financial reality at the time was truly impossible for him. He was trying to at least keep the stars together for a few years. The role players, one by one, were gone. Within the next year, I'd be joined by Bob Errey, Troy Loney, and Bryan Trottier as former members of the Penguins. Losing a lot of successful role players isn't a good way to win Stanley Cups, but Craig didn't have a choice. I understood this. I have so much respect for Craig as a man and as a general manager. He was the best. Truly the best, a Hall of Famer. He did everything he could, but my time with the Penguins was through.

I signed with the Rangers. Holy shit, was training camp uncomfortable. No one talked to me at first. No one. It was so damn awkward.

We had training camp in Glens Falls, New York. For most of camp, I was an outcast for the first time in my life. It sucked. But then, on the last day of camp, something unexpected happened from the most unexpected source.

Adam Graves, the biggest villain of them all, approached me. "We're all going to dinner," he said. "Why don't you join us?"

So I accepted the offer. Graves was at the dinner. Brian Leetch, Mike Richter, Tie Domi too. The conversation quickly turned to the rivalry between the Penguins and the Rangers. I sensed just a bit of hostility.

"We all fucking hated you," Graves said to me. "But you're one of us now. We think you're a good guy."

I remember thinking, *Wow, what a great compliment. You all hated me for the right reason. Thank you for hating me so much.*

During this time, I also got to know Mark Messier. Damn. What a man, what a captain. All the things you've heard about him over the years are true. He had these captain qualities that were pretty special. He had an awareness of everyone on the team. He knew that you were only as good as your weakest link, and so he made sure that everyone, from the best player on the team to the worst, was taken care of. It didn't matter who you were, how much money you made, when you were drafted. He would treat you well and treat you with respect. I'd hear him say stuff like, "Hey, want to come to lunch with me? Hey, do you need a place to stay? You can stay at my place." The captain Sid has become reminds me of Messier. Same kind of leadership. He has the same way of taking care of people. He always had the pulse of the team in the palm of his hand.

But man, it was weird playing for the Rangers. They were always taking shots at Mario, and I didn't like being on the opposite side of that. I was on the ice in 1988 when David Shaw slashed Mario in the throat, which triggered such a huge brawl. Then there was the nasty playoff series. And it all spilled over into the 1992–93 season.

There's one moment from that season I remember well. We were playing Mario and the Penguins in New York. And we had some guys that were really taking runs at Mario. It was getting pretty nasty. To make matters worse, we sucked that year, and they were the best team in the league. Finally, the Penguins had enough of us taking runs at the big guy. During a TV timeout, I was sitting there on the bench when I noticed that Tocchet had skated over to Messier. Now, keep in mind, these two were friends. They had played together for Canada in the 1987 Canada Cup and had played on All-Star teams together. So, there was major respect on both sides.

"Hey Mark," Tocchet said to Messier during a TV timeout. "You know I have a lot of respect for you. But I'm going to tell you something right now. If one more of your guys takes a run at Mario, I'm going to fucking kill you."

Messier didn't flinch. He skated over to the bench, looked at all of us, and gave the "knock it off" gesture with his hand by his throat. I guess no one liked to fuck with Rick Tocchet.

But Jesus, what a miserable season for me. I only played in 55 games. I was banged up and was also a healthy scratch in a few games. I only finished with six goals and 20 points. Everything was a mess that year in New York. We didn't even make the playoffs after the Rangers had won the Presidents' Trophy the season before. I played like shit. Head coach Roger Neilson got fired. Leetch broke his ankle when he fell in a snow bank. The team was a total train wreck, to be quite honest.

One memory I have of that season perfectly summarizes everything I was feeling. That was the season when pretty much all teams started using charter flights. We were on a flight back to New York after another shitty game, and I started talking with a flight attendant. She remembered me from the Penguins the previous season. "You'll never guess this," she said. "But after we drop you guys off, we're actually going to pick up the Penguins and take them home."

A light went off in my head.

"I need you to do me a favor," I said to her.

I grabbed one of those barf bags they have on planes and a pen. I wrote a note.

Dear Craig,
Scrappy, speedy winger available. Would love to come back to the 'Burgh.
—Bourquey

I don't think she ever gave him the note, but I suppose it probably wouldn't have mattered. They couldn't afford me a few months earlier, so I'm sure they couldn't at that point. But dammit, I had to try.

I'd say I hated that season more than any in my hockey career. Everything was bad except for my paycheck. And hey, that paycheck was great; don't get me wrong. And living in New York had its perks for sure. But the fact of the matter is, I wasn't happy—for multiple reasons.

I wasn't quite the same player starting the season, and I wasn't sure why.

The guys were nice to me after a while, but it wasn't the same as playing in Pittsburgh, where we had become family.

I was getting more injuries at that stage in my career.

And my wife, Julie, didn't want to live in New York at all.

That last part was becoming a problem. You must understand that Julie is a California girl. She loved the sunshine, loved the warm climate in California. She wasn't wild about Pittsburgh, and she sure as hell didn't want to live in New York.

Put bluntly, it was the season from hell.

Watching the Penguins get stunned in the second round by the Islanders didn't make me feel any better. I hated to see them go down like that. Those were my guys, great champions who should have won more Cups. But they didn't. And my life was getting more and more miserable in New York.

The bond you form when you win a Stanley Cup is something that I can't properly explain. You would do anything for those guys for the rest of your life, put it that way. That's the bond I felt with the Penguins. I was an undrafted nobody and they took a shot on me, believed in me. They trained me throughout the minors for years. They gave me the opportunity to become a champion. I had so much loyalty to that franchise, and I knew it was reciprocated. They were just out of money and dealing with that reality was difficult. The good times were through.

These were rough days for me. And they were about to get worse.

CHAPTER 14
DIVORCE AND A MISSED OPPORTUNITY

I started my second season with the Rangers as a healthy scratch on a regular basis. It was pretty discouraging. I had worked hard to finally make it with the Penguins. By the end of the 1987–88 season, I had finally become a regular. It's not easy when you're undrafted. There's a stigma there. You've got to work a little harder, prove your worth a little more. I'd done that and was proud of it.

So, sitting in the press box many a night in Madison Square Garden wasn't exactly my idea of a good time. That said, it wasn't all bad. Manhattan isn't the worst place in the world, and my ego wasn't totally destroyed. You have to keep some things in mind.

The Rangers had more money than God.

There was no salary cap at this time.

The Rangers were obsessed with winning the Cup for the first time since 1940.

Thus, I wasn't exactly sitting in the press box with bums. Hell, my roommate was Eddie Olczyk, and he was a healthy scratch on most nights as well. Edzo scored 342 NHL goals and was the third overall pick, two behind Mario. He was still pretty young at that time, too. That's how good those Rangers were. Eddie, who was in his late twenties, in his prime, wasn't good enough to play on most nights.

The Rangers had so much money, they just didn't care. They were obsessed with winning and were more than happy to buy a championship if that's what it took. If you think about it, the economics of the game were really strange back then. For the players, I guess it was a good thing teams like the Rangers existed. They were willing to spend whatever amount it took. That's great. But from a fan's standpoint, I'm sure it was a little different. Teams like the Penguins, who had developed some talent and made wise deals to acquire even more, couldn't really keep their teams together. Think about the players the Penguins had to let go in the years after the Cup: me, Troy Loney, Bob Errey, Kevin Stevens. There were others, too. Craig did everything he could to keep that team together, but he had no chance because of teams like the Rangers.

So, here's what was happening: I hated that I wasn't playing, but I liked my paycheck. I didn't mind living in New York, but Julie hated it, so my marriage was crumbling.

Then, in January, I get a call from my agent.

"There are teams interested in you," he said. "I can get you out of there so you can play."

Now wait just a minute. Sure, I wanted to play. And sure, I wasn't so happy with the situation. But I knew the Rangers were winning the Cup that year. There wasn't a doubt in my mind. So, I told my agent, "Don't fucking call Neil. Please. Let's worry about it in the summer. I'm still getting my money. And I'm one injury away from being on the ice and playing for the Cup again. Please don't make the call."

That's the thing about the Cup. Maybe it wouldn't have been the same in New York because, in my heart, I was always going to be a member of the Penguins. But there is an allure to winning the Cup that I really can't explain. It drives you. It's so powerful. So, if you think you're going to have a chance to win it, you'll do anything for it, even if that means staying in a shitty situation.

So I kept doing the healthy scratch thing. Edzo and I were having fun, at least. What a great guy, a great roommate. It was a similar situation for both of us, but we got through it together. Then it was trade deadline day. We were in Calgary. It was almost 1:00 PM there, which was the deadline. I was in my room with Edzo and Mike Hartman. We were all nervous as hell. We had been healthy scratches, but we didn't want to be traded. We knew how close we were to winning a Cup and we had all decided that we wanted to stick it out, give the Rangers some depth. When 1:00 PM came and went, and none of us had been traded, we were fucking ecstatic. We were literally high-fiving each other and shit.

Then, the phone rang. I got a sick feeling in my stomach. Edzo said, "Bourquey, it's Neil. He wants to talk with you."

This is how the conversation went:

"Hi Neil. Where did you trade me to?"

"Bourquey, we want to thank you for your service to the Rangers."

"Where the fuck did you trade me to, Neil?"

"Bourquey, you've been traded to the Ottawa Senators. Your flight leaves in two hours. There's a car waiting for you at your hotel."

"Ottawa? Fucking Ottawa? Thanks a fucking lot, Neil. Fuck off. That just ruined my marriage."

"Bourquey, Bourquey, I can't control that."

I called Julie and told her I was going to Ottawa. She wasn't amused, which I knew would be the case. She was a total California girl. She wasn't in love with Pittsburgh or New York. Didn't like the cold weather. Didn't like much about anything in New York. I knew she wasn't coming to Ottawa, and she never did.

We sold our house in Westchester. I was traded in March. I was divorced a few months later. Just like that. Of course, before we actually decided to get divorced, I made a last-ditch effort to make her happy. We bought a house in Anaheim. She spent a bajillion fucking dollars on furnishing the new house. Meanwhile, I was miserable in Ottawa. It was cold. It was still basically an expansion team. All my career, I'd played for great teams. And, even though I was happy to be getting a regular shift, I wasn't happy playing for a shit team.

A little while later, I got hurt in Ottawa. So I wasn't playing at all. I was just driving to the game one night when Julie calls me. She was living in California; I was in freaking Ottawa. She said, "I think we should get a divorce." I said, "Absolutely." So she said, "You get a lawyer, and I'll get a lawyer."

At this point in time, my life completely sucked. The team sucked. I was starting to suck as a player. I was getting divorced and, even though I was still making my Rangers money, I was losing a lot of that money to her.

Listen, I know what my reputation was during my playing days. I was a party guy. I loved women. And it's all true. But I've done a lot in the last 10 or 15 years to try and change that reputation a little bit. You need to understand that I wasn't the type to cheat on a woman. I really wasn't. A lot of hockey players were, no question. But I was never like that. Dating two women at once? No thanks. That would have been far, far too difficult. I wasn't interested in that, anyway. If I was guilty of anything, it was not ending a bad relationship before I started another. It's not like I was trying to do shit behind women's backs, though. I never, ever was like that and I kind of resent that reputation, to be honest.

But anyway, my life was in the shitter. I was hurt. I was lonely. So, what did I do? I started hanging out in strip clubs in Ottawa. No harm, really. I wasn't looking for a woman in a strip club. It was just good entertainment. I could walk into a place, look at naked women, have a beer, and otherwise be totally left alone. It was essentially what I was looking for at the time. However, it turns out I wasn't alone. You'll never believe this.

Julie had decided to hire a private investigator to trail me. I swear to God. The divorce wasn't finalized yet, and she wanted to get me for every dollar she could. This guy followed me all over creation trying to figure out what I was up to.

Now, you might be wondering, *How did you know about this?* One day, I picked up my mail. And I noticed this huge envelope from an attorney. It was addressed to Julie, but it came to my house. I'm not a jealous person. I'm not nosy. I'm really not. But something told me to open it, so I did. And wouldn't you know it, what I saw was a very detailed report of her private investigator's findings. I couldn't believe it. I was in fucking shock. The best part is, he had absolutely nothing on me. Nothing. It actually said, "He's a really good guy. I don't know why you hired me to follow this person around. I followed him everywhere. He went into some strip clubs, but he was by himself the whole time. Just drinking some beers. No girls were around him. He didn't talk with anyone. He sat by himself. He looked lonely. There's absolutely nothing wrong with this guy, nothing going on with this guy. I've talked with everyone about this guy. This is a guy with a lot of character, a lot of work ethic. Everyone seems to respect this guy and think that he's a good person. There is absolutely nothing going on with this guy. Nothing at all. Again, I'm not sure why you even hired me to follow this person around. He went to strip clubs but didn't do anything wrong in these settings. This isn't a bad guy at all, and there's nothing I can do to help you out."

What did I do with this information? I gave Julie a call.

I called her up and said, "Hey, Donkey. You probably should change your address, because your private detective report came to my house."

She didn't know what to say. She was in shock. It was great. She said something like, "Oh, so I guess you know." I responded, "Yeah, I guess you could say I know."

She put an enormous amount of effort into her body, I'll give her that. She had a lot of physical assets, and she rather enjoyed showing them off.

It almost got to the point that it was a little embarrassing. Back in the old days at the Igloo, the family section was in C-2. As I've mentioned, I didn't like looking into the crowd during games. It made me nervous, uncomfortable. You name it. I rarely did it. But when your wife is involved, it changes things. She loved to wait until

TV timeouts or breaks in play before she'd take her seat. Everyone else was usually seated before the game began, but not her. To her, it was a New York City fashion show or something. I would hear a noise and look up during breaks. I'd see 20 guys standing up giving her a standing ovation as she walked past. It was something else. She'd literally be wearing six-inch heels, dressed to the nines, cleavage on full display. I would honestly say that the other wives and girlfriends were a little intimidated by her because of the way she dressed. They had absolutely no clue what to make of her. It was showtime for her as far as she was concerned. I think the rest of them were there to be supportive, to watch the hockey game and have a good time. But she definitely enjoyed the attention that her body got her. However, it's not like she didn't want to be friends with the wives and girlfriends. She wanted to. She actually made an effort. They just didn't know what to make of her. I think Nathalie, Mario Lemieux's then-girlfriend, now wife, felt sorry for her, to be honest. She befriended her. Nathalie is really great, and she went above and beyond to make Julie feel a little more comfortable, to help her fit in with everyone a little bit. But I wouldn't say that anyone got totally comfortable with her, nor did she ever get totally comfortable with everyone else.

I spent a lot of time thinking about my marriage to Julie and where it all went wrong. My family life growing up was a train wreck. I always held my dad responsible for a lot of our problems and, as a result, I had a very strong desire to provide something that my dad never did. And I'd started pondering my own life, my own decisions. I had done a lot. I'd won the Stanley Cup twice, developed a successful career. I was popular. People liked me. The only thing I really felt that was missing was a family, having kids. This was part of the problem. I was under the impression that Julie would want to have kids, settle down, have a family with me. But after we got married, she made it quite clear to me that she didn't want kids. She wanted to keep doing her bikini contests. She wanted to keep her body in perfect form. She was younger than me, and I guess she wasn't quite ready for that. And that was her right, of course. It's not like I was ever telling her what to do. But we were definitely on different pages in how we envisioned the ideal scenario for the next few years. It was a huge problem. And of course, like I said, she was a few years younger than me.

But upon reflection, this was a very difficult time in my life.

My career in the NHL was starting to fade, and I knew it. I had kept myself in good shape and I was still pretty young, but the game is hard. And I never felt like I was quite the same player after leaving the Penguins. That happened a lot with guys in Pittsburgh. There was something in the water that made you a better player when you played for the Penguins, I swear.

Injuries were starting to build up for me. My personal life was a mess. And I missed playing on a great hockey team. It was a hell of a struggle for me, and it's probably fair to say that I was becoming a little depressed. A few years earlier, I had been partying on the river all summer with the Stanley Cup. Julie and I were happy and having a blast. I was starting to make more money. I thought we'd win a million Cups in a row and that I'd always be wearing the Black and Gold. I was convinced of these things. Then, I realized that the NHL is an unforgiving business and that life doesn't always work out the way you think it will.

This can be quite a rude awakening for a person and, for me, it certainly was. The early '90s were without question the best time of my life, but as the decade started to move on, I felt my life and everything I had known starting to slip away from me.

It happened to a lot of us from those Penguins teams. Mario's health had gotten so bad. The year after I left, he was diagnosed with cancer. He heroically returned and still won the scoring title, but all the radiation treatments—and the back problems that never went away—were starting to take a toll. He was already contemplating retirement by the mid-90s.

Kevin Stevens was getting pretty deep into addiction by this time. None of us knew it, though. Like the rest of us, Artie always enjoyed an adult beverage. But he started doing cocaine in 1993 and it led to other heavy drugs. He's one of the greatest humans I've ever known, and I love him dearly. He should be in the Hall of Fame. But he was never the same player after the drug use began.

Tommy Barrasso was never the same goalie after the early '90s and, for reasons I'll never understand, became more and more abrasive as the years went by. He was never friendly, but he kept getting worse and worse in that regard.

Joey Mullen was getting older and injuries had really slowed him down. Even though Jagr would go on to be the world's best player in the late '90s, he was dealing with groin injuries that really slowed him down for a period of time. Ronnie Francis had a few great years left in him and is one of the best two-way centers ever, but I'd say he probably peaked in the early '90s as a player.

It's funny how it all worked out. Once our team started to separate, a lot of guys still had great years and did great things on and off the rink. But I'd argue that none of us was ever quite the same. Even though we were a group of strong personalities in a lot of ways, and a group of independent people, I would suggest that we all kind of needed each other to be at our absolute best.

Damn, did I ever find that out the hard way. As the years started to move on, I found myself missing the Pittsburgh Penguins more and more. My career, and my life, never quite felt right when I wasn't a part of that organization, of that family.

CHAPTER 15

THE FEELING
OF DEATH

I was getting pretty depressed in the summer of 1994. Don't let anyone tell you that money buys you happiness, because it most certainly doesn't.

Those last two years in Pittsburgh kind of represented the top of the mountain for me. I played a key role on back-to-back Stanley Cup championship teams and, aside from that, there was just something about the guys on that team. We were a bunch of brothers. I loved living in Pittsburgh so much. I was happily married. Honestly, I had no choice but to leave Pittsburgh when I did, but life was never quite the same.

And by 1994, it was really getting bad. My marriage was down the toilet, I was away from Pittsburgh, I was away from another good team in New York, and slowly but surely, I felt my body starting to break down. At this point, I was on the wrong side of 30 and I was starting to feel it in my bones. I was playing for a shit team in Ottawa.

Yet, I was determined. I still had two years remaining on a fairly lucrative contract, and I knew I could still play. I just needed to work a little harder than I had in the past. That was the whole key. My game was always rooted in my ability to skate. I could still fly, but for the following season, I wanted to be at my very best in terms of conditioning. While the rest of the country was watching the O.J. Simpson drama in the summer of '94, I was working my ass off like never before. I was working out every day like a madman. The trade to Ottawa and, really, everything about the previous two years, had me upset. When you're in the second half of your career, you start thinking about your legacy, how fans will remember you. All that stuff. And hell, you also want another contract once your current once expires.

So, as the summer dragged on, I was feeling better and better. I was in the best shape of my life. There was a chance of a lockout for the 1994–95 season, but I wasn't even thinking about it at the time. I was just focused on myself and being the best player I could be. Even if the Senators sucked, I was going to have a good season.

Before training camp was set to start, I decided to have one weekend of fun in late August. It's always good to get away for a bit before camp. I had been so depressed for the months leading up to this summer but, at this point, I was starting to feel like myself again. When you're me, though, you always prioritize having fun. When the NHL schedule is released every season, I always pick out those Florida trips first. And Vegas, Montreal, Chicago. You know, the fun places. I'm the kind of guy who never met a good time he didn't like. I'm like that to this very day, and I was sure as hell like that back then. So before the grind of the season was to begin, I needed to have some fun.

I decided to head to the outdoors for my little trip. This is a part of my personality, my passion. Hell, remember when I said we were going to take the Cup out on the river and party all summer? The fact is, I was a man of my word. I spent the summer of 1991 on the river with the Cup. A company called Ski Supreme contacted a friend of mine and asked if he knew of any Pittsburgh Penguins who might be interested in a custom-made Penguins boat to put on the water. I had the damn thing docked in the Strip District all summer. At the time, I had taken up barefoot waterskiing. It's not easy, but my God, was it fun. As my career elapsed, I developed more and more of an appreciation for the outdoors. I loved being in the water, I loved mountains, you name it.

Julie and I had made friends who lived in Utah. We used to get into some real adventures. So, for this little trip, I decided to go to Lake Powell. It's north of the Grand Canyon, a really beautiful place. I just wanted to have a guilt-free weekend—go out with some friends, drink some beers, go out on the water. It sounded like a perfect weekend getaway before the grind of the season began. Little did I know, it would almost end my life.

I met my friends there on a Friday afternoon. It was going to be a fun night, and I was in a good mood because of my work that summer. I was proud. I was running hills, doing all kinds of stuff to get in the best shape of my life. When I got to Lake Powell, I saw how beautiful it was. The rugged terrain everywhere. It was great. But then I started thinking, *You've worked so hard all summer. Get a good run in before you have your fun.*

Then, as I was taking a run, I noticed a mountain. I was just wearing a pair of shorts, no shirt. It was hot as hell. I start thinking about this mountain. From what I had always heard, climbing mountains makes for an unbelievable workout. I had some time to kill; everyone else was just hanging out and drinking. So fuck it. I decided I was going to climb the mountain.

This area was called Lone Rock Canyon and, let me tell you, I felt pretty alone climbing this mountain. The area I was climbing was about 500 feet. I made it to the 350-foot mark, and I was loving it. I had the deep burn going in my legs. My arms were getting a good workout, too. It was beautiful. My friends were in a houseboat way below me, waving. I was waving back, putting on a little show for them. I was going higher and higher and then, all of a sudden, I almost slipped and fell backward. That wouldn't have ended well. At that point, I said to myself, *Stop being a fucking idiot. Go back down the mountain. Enough is enough.*

I started navigating the mountain at that point, looking for a safer route to make my way down. The problem was, there weren't any safe routes on this mountain. The whole thing was dangerous, and obviously I never should have been up there. Still, I had to find my way back down, whether I liked it or not. Slowly but surely, I started descending. I was pretty scared. I knew that I was in a bad spot, that I was going to have to rely on all of my natural God-given athleticism and strength to make my way back down. It gave me an appreciation for people who scale mountains on a regular basis. Maybe they're crazy. Maybe they're brave. Maybe they're both.

I was starting to feel a little better. I was making my way toward the bottom, planning landing areas one step at a time. I was cursing myself the whole way down, mumbling to myself that I was being an idiot. All my life, I lived in the fast lane and occasionally did some incredibly stupid shit. But this was new territory, even for me. Luckily, though, I was starting to make some good progress.

Then, my life changed forever.

I shifted my weight to go left, and when I did, everything underneath me crumbled. I started falling, and falling, and falling. It's the last thing I remember. I remember falling through the air, but I don't recall the impact.

I fell 40 feet to the ground, which of course knocked me out cold. It's funny, the things you think when you might be dying. If you haven't been there, if you haven't been in that situation, I don't really know if you can understand. Everything slows down for a moment and you think very clearly. As I was falling through the air, I knew that I might be dead. I had to confront that immediately, and I did. Believe it or not, I made my peace with it. I remember thinking to myself, *At least I don't have kids, so there won't be kids that have to grow up without their father. It's been a hell of a ride. If this is how it ends, then this is how it ends.*

I was out for a while, and I was lying at the bottom of the mountain for about an hour by myself before the people in the houseboat realized that I had disappeared and went looking for me. When I came to, I knew I was in deep trouble. I couldn't see. My eyes were swollen completely shut. I remember taking my thumb and index finger and trying to pry open my eyes. I went into shock at the same time. I'll never forget the heat on my face and all the blood leaving it. That's when you know you might be dying, when you feel that. I was so scraped up in every imaginable way. The skin off the back of my hands was completely gone. It was a strange feeling, and not a good one. The pain I was in was almost indescribable. My nostrils got cut open something horrible. My nose was barely hanging on to my face. It was a freaky feeling. My nose felt like it wasn't there, so my face felt wide open in a way. My face just wouldn't stop bleeding. You're lying there, and you really can't move or speak. You're just waiting to hear someone's voice. I knew I could die there.

Finally, I heard people yelling. They had found me. I can still hear someone saying, "Stay calm. You're in trouble. We're going to get you a park ranger."

It's bad enough that I had just experienced a life-or-death situation. I mean, that's enough to get your attention, and not in a good way. But then I started thinking to myself that I'm not exactly in New York or Pittsburgh. Or Ottawa. Or L.A. Or anywhere that might have an actual fucking hospital. I wanted to be in the middle of nowhere that weekend. I wanted to get away from gyms, from hockey rinks, from civilization, from my life. And now, I was on the verge of losing my life, and there was no way there was a hospital anywhere close by. I kept thinking about how isolated I was and how long it would be before medical attention could come my way.

My buddy who found me got in his boat and went to find a park ranger. It was so damn isolated. It took forever, but he finally found people. Thank God. Meanwhile, I was still lying there, wondering if I'm going to live. You think about everything. Your family. Hockey. You name it. When they found me, all I could think about was whether I was going to live. And what an adventure it was.

It took them four hours to get me out of there. Four hours. Two hundred and forty minutes. Or, if you prefer, 14,400 seconds. I suffered through every one of them. It wasn't a very comfortable escape, even though I'm eternally grateful for it. It took eight paramedics to pick me up and get me out on a gurney. After four hours, they managed to get me into a basket. A helicopter came to get me. They hooked me up and got me into the helicopter. At that point, you pretty much feel like you're in a movie. In no way did it feel like real life. The helicopter took me to Flagstaff, Arizona.

For the first time in my life, I began to feel claustrophobic. I was absolutely freaking out while I was in the helicopter. Literally, I felt like I was buried alive. They had my arms and legs all strapped down and my head was immobilized. I kept asking the people in the helicopter if I could get up because, even though I didn't exactly feel like running a marathon, the feeling of being trapped was actually worse than the considerable discomfort I was feeling. They very politely told me that I wasn't allowed to move.

I couldn't see. I could barely move. But I wanted to move in the worst way.

When I got to the hospital, the doctor gave me a rather extensive laundry list of my injuries:

- Broken neck in five places
- Three-inch fracture to my skull
- Two broken cheekbones
- Broken nose
- Broken forehead
- We didn't even talk about it, but of course I had a horrible concussion, too

The doctor had to stitch together all the skin that was dangling off me. My face had skin hanging from places where it wasn't supposed to be hanging. My hands had no skin at all. I'm glad I couldn't get up to look at myself in the mirror. That vision probably would have haunted me forever.

You know what the amazing thing was? I never had to have surgery. The doctor thought about surgery on my forehead, but he ultimately decided that it wasn't necessary. I can still remember the doctor asking me if I could wiggle my fingers or toes. Luckily, I could.

Then he uttered words that I'll never forget.

"You should be paralyzed or dead," he said. "I just looked at your MRI. It's a good thing you're a professional athlete."

He went on to tell me that someone who wasn't in my kind of shape—someone who wasn't an athlete, essentially—never would have survived that kind of fall. It's funny when I think about it now. I was in the best shape of my life and, because I wanted to maintain that shape, I felt like climbing that mountain. Life doesn't make any sense sometimes, to say the least.

I was in the hospital for a while, as you would imagine. After a few days, I was starting to move around a little bit. At that point, I could finally exhale, because I knew I was going to survive. That was the first step. I was so motivated to get back into great playing shape and put a few more great seasons together before the injury. After the fall, I was still eager for that, but I was probably more interested in just making it back to the league. When you're young, when you're a good athlete and winning championships, you completely take life for granted. You think it will never end, that you'll have a career until you're 40 and then retire to the good life. You really do think that way. The idea of something like what happened to me doesn't cross your mind. When it happens, you don't know what to do. You don't have a clue. You just know that something horrible has happened and you attempt, day by day, to put your life and your career back together. It's daunting as hell.

I try not to think about that day too often. It's not a pleasant memory and, in general, it wasn't a very pleasant time in my life. I was trying to do the right thing. I was trying to be an adult, to get myself in ideal shape, to truly devote myself to my profession. In that regard, yeah, I was starting to grow up. But deep down, to my core, I was still a wild man. I enjoyed living the life. I enjoyed being spontaneous. It was always kind of my thing. What the hell is more spontaneous than deciding to climb a random mountain? Yeah, that was me. Living the life served me well but, even as I was starting to behave a little better and take my career a little more seriously, I almost lost my life because I was living the life.

So, there I was. I was 32 years old and I could barely move. I just wanted to get back to playing hockey again, to being myself again. I was so damn happy to be alive. Trust me, I was. But I also wasn't happy with my life.

Getting back to the NHL quickly became the next thing on my mind. And I was determined to get back. But the NHL being the NHL, it wasn't going to be as simple as it sounds.

CHAPTER 16
GETTING
BACK UP

For the next couple months, I was confined to a bed. All my life, I rather enjoyed being in bed. But not now. It was the worst time of my life.

The Senators decided to fly their team doctor in to look at me and to assess my condition. Thankfully, my career wasn't over. There would be some considerably tough times in the coming months, but the doctor said I'd be able to resume my playing career, which of course was a major relief.

While I'd be able to play again, I knew I wouldn't be good to go for a while. But as it would turn out, neither would the NHL.

What was bad news for the hockey world was a breath of fresh air for me. The 1994–95 season didn't begin until late January because of a lockout. Thank God. I wouldn't have been able to play until December at the very earliest, and I didn't particularly like the idea of missing a large chunk of the season because I fell off a damn mountain. I was resigned to the reality that I had probably won the Stanley Cup for the final time. In the back of my mind, I knew anything was possible. I knew I could be traded to a contender. In the deepest portions of my heart, I was always hoping Craig would pick up the phone and bring me home. But I knew it wasn't financially reasonable. And I sure as hell knew the Ottawa Senators weren't winning the Cup any time soon. Or any time, period.

Back in Pittsburgh, things were never quite the same after our team started to break up. The Penguins were shocked in 1993 against the Islanders, losing in Game 7. I still remember watching that game, feeling shocked, just like all of Pittsburgh. The following season saw the Rangers win the Cup, and you'd have thought they'd be forced to go through the Penguins at some point, but it never happened. Instead, the Penguins went out with a whimper that season, falling to the Washington Capitals—yes, really—in the first round of the playoffs. I knew the Penguins well enough to know that something wasn't right. The band was starting to break up, and I knew it wasn't getting back together. Mario, in fact, had decided to skip the 1994–95 season entirely. His body was still completely fatigued from the radiation treatments that were required to defeat his cancer 18 months earlier. Plus, his back was still a mess. I knew from sharing a locker room with him for so many years that Mario played in extraordinary amounts of pain. It had finally caught up to him. It's amazing, really, to think that the greatest hockey player of all time would just need a break from hockey at age 29. How sad. I grew up watching Bobby Orr play in Boston, and it was much the same for him. Hell, his career was pretty much over at that stage. I hated it as a kid for Bobby, and Mario was my friend and my longtime teammate, so I really hated seeing him struggle with it.

I always figured Mario would come back again at some point and, as fate would have it, he still had MVPs and scoring titles in his future. When you're great, you're great. But I knew the Penguins weren't really great anymore, and I knew that I didn't really have a place to call home. Any dreams I had of someday returning to the Penguins were pretty much gone, and I had to accept that, even if it wasn't the easiest reality for me. So, what was my plan? Pretty simple, really. Recover from the injuries and close out my NHL career with some dignity, maybe get one or two more contracts, and finish on my terms, with plenty of money in the bank.

Sure, it sucked being in Ottawa. There were no Marios in that lineup. It was cold. My accountant was always bitching because living in Canada was such a financial hit due to their taxes. But I still had that dream of being an NHL player, and I wasn't going to let it die. I still had a contract, too.

The lockout was such a blessing. Even though I was functional enough after the accident, I was confined to bed for a couple months. I think anyone who has been in a similar situation will tell you that the most brutal part of the recovery is just lying around, being bored out of your mind, sitting in bed. That was me in September and October 1994. I wasn't really allowed to do anything. I couldn't drive yet. I couldn't hit the gym. I didn't have much energy to do a damn thing anyway. But the boredom was overwhelming. I'm the kind of guy who can get bored pretty quickly to begin with. I require a good bit of stimulation in my day-to-day life. If I have a few days off, instead of sitting down and taking it easy, I'm much more likely to go golfing in Florida for a few days or to do something with my kids. It's how I'm wired. That fall was horrible.

But finally, November came. At that point, I was feeling much better, more like myself. I was actually able to get my ass back into the gym, which was a great feeling. Unfortunately, a lot of the work I had done before the injury was lost, but I tried not to think about it that way. I had been in the best shape of my life before and I was determined to get back to something in that neighborhood by the time the NHL season was set to begin.

The season began in late January and, like I said, we were horrible. There was some young talent coming through the system in Ottawa and, in fact, by the end of the decade the Senators were legitimate contenders. But not when I was there. We went 9–34–5 that season. Yeah, you read that right. And hell, it could have been worse, as we somehow won five of our late-season games that year. How, I'll never know.

Playing on that rotten of a team is very difficult for anyone, let alone for someone who played on Stanley Cup teams. You feel a sense of depression when you're driving to the rink. As an athlete, you're programmed to always believe you're invincible, to think you're going to win every game you play. That's always how you're trained, from the time you're a little kid until you become a professional. That mentality is never supposed to change. At the same time, if you have a brain and any sense of realism, you know that's not always the case. And if you ever needed more evidence that such a belief isn't realistic, try playing for an expansion team back then. Yeah, I know what Vegas did, but that was 2018, not the 1990s. It was different then, let me tell you.

By late April, we were 4–32–5. We'd play against the elite teams like the Devils, Penguins, or Rangers and just get embarrassed. Even though we ultimately won nine games that season, we only beat four teams: the Islanders, Flyers, Lightning, and Sabres, none of whom were especially good at that point in time. It was that bad. And for me, it was about to get worse.

It was April 24, 1995. We were at home against the Florida Panthers. I mean, really, how irrelevant does that sound? You get the picture. I was in the middle of a regular shift, and all of a sudden, I hit a rut in the ice. Oh my God, the pain I felt. There went my ACL. Major surgery. Total reconstruction of the ACL. I couldn't believe it. In eight months, I had gone from being in the best shape of my life to falling off a mountain, being stuck in bed for two months, and then blowing my knee in the most meaningless game of my life.

The '90s were really the highest of the highs and the lowest of the lows for me. It felt like torture by the middle of the decade. Don't ever let someone tell you that money buys happiness, because I'm living proof that it does not. I was rolling in cash at that point in my life, but the fact of the matter was, I was lonely and unhappy. Winning, especially at the highest of levels in professional sports, is so addictive. It feels better than anything. It's better than money, better than sex, better than traveling the world. I swear to God, there's nothing like the feeling of playing for a great hockey team, knowing there's going to be a sellout crowd every night, and knowing that beautiful Cup will be waiting for you at the end of your journey. In my life, there's been nothing like that feeling. By April of 1995, it was so incredibly far away, I couldn't believe it. It's like I was living in an alternate universe. Once upon a time, I was the guy partying on the river all summer. Now, I was rehabbing a knee injury all day, every day. My face didn't quite feel right. And I was 33, knowing full well that my NHL career was probably coming to an end.

Along the way, I was absolutely spending money like an idiot. There's a pressure that comes with being a professional athlete. You aren't supposed to drive an ordinary car. You've got to have a BMW or something even fancier. When you go out to dinner with friends, you're always the one who picks up the check. When you're going on a trip with friends, you're always the one who pays for the hotel rooms and the transportation. It's just the way it is. You know you're making a ton of money, probably way more than your friends, so you end paying for everything. I've always been the guy who picks up every check. It's part of my personality, and it was part of the responsibility that I felt. So, I kept doing this over and over again during that summer. I still had one more year remaining on my Rangers contract, so I knew the money would be rolling in for a while. But in the back of my mind, I knew some problems in my personal life were starting to mount.

I was lonely as hell. I had failed at marriage. My body was hurting. For a hockey player, I was getting old. I always wanted to be a dad and didn't have any kids to share life with. I was ripping through money like an idiot. I was missing Pittsburgh. I was missing the taste of victory.

It wasn't how I imagined my career turning out that damn day I signed with the Rangers. But in retrospect, I don't have any regrets. What was I to do? The other big offer I received was from San Jose. The Sharks were an expansion team, too, and cost of living is just as brutal in that neck of the woods as it was in New York and Ottawa.

So, I signed for a lot of money with the best team I could sign with. Isn't that what anyone else would do?

Sometimes, though, life doesn't turn out the way you expect it to. That's the situation I was in as I faced the longest rehab period of my life. Back then, ACL surgery kept you out for around a year. I was determined to make it back before then, but I knew it would be a second miserable summer for me.

I was spending time all over the place back then. I had a place in Ottawa, but I still liked going home to Boston a good bit. And, of course, Pittsburgh was really my home by this point in time. That's where so many of my friends were. Over time, I realized that while I was perfectly comfortable in Boston and while I'm pretty good at fitting in anywhere, Pittsburgh was always home for me. It's always where I felt most relaxed. Remember, I dealt with nervousness and anxiety my entire life. But I found Pittsburgh had a calming effect on me that other places didn't. So, I'd still sneak back from time to time, because it's what made me feel best.

But by the time the 1995–96 season rolled around, Pittsburgh was pretty far away. And my glory days as a player were feeling pretty far away, too.

CHAPTER 17
THE LAST
HURRAH

Being a professional athlete affords you many privileges. Being honest about your health isn't one of them.

In the early stages of the 1995–96 season, I was still feeling pain in my knee. I shouldn't have been playing yet. It's a major injury we're talking about, and I had a lot of wear on those tires. But when you're an athlete, there's nothing worse than sitting out. Nothing. And remember, I was still making money on the last year of my big deal. Sure, you're still happy to be collecting paychecks. But it's not a pleasant feeling to know you're making a lot of money and not helping your hockey team, even if it's a bad hockey team. So, what did I do? I lied through my teeth to the team doctors.

You feel better, Bourquey?

Oh yeah, sure.

You positive, Bourquey?

Absolutely, I'm ready to play.

It was like that, and it wasn't the smartest thing for me. But I wanted to be back in the NHL and, truth be told, I was pretty proud of myself for making it back that season. I had been through an awful lot during the previous 18 months, but I was back in the NHL.

Back when I played, things were so different. I'm not saying hockey players aren't tough now, because of course they are. You don't block shots the way they do and absorb the constant physical punishment they do if you don't possess some toughness. There's no doubting this. But things were so much different. My God. Back then, especially in the '80s, if you had a concussion and missed more than a week, you were considered soft. That's just the way it was. That was the mindset, and if you think about it, it's a pretty scary thing. It must have been especially brutal for the guys who fought all the time, the true NHL heavyweights. There were fights every game and those guys could really throw them. Those were big, scary men just beating the shit out of each other. It was a concussion fest, no doubt.

But you didn't really see people missing time due to concussions then. Oh, maybe a game or two, but players literally almost never missed more than a week with a concussion. Think about that. Think about how scary that is, knowing what we know now. It makes you cringe just thinking about it. The sport has changed so much. But I started playing the game seriously in the '70s and broke into pro hockey in the '80s. That was the dream. That was everything. And I don't care how good you were, if an NHL team—or an OHL team, college team, or minor league team, for that matter—thought you were soft, you were screwed. You had no chance. They literally didn't want anything to do with you unless you were some kind of superstar. Hell, you couldn't be a superstar and be soft back then because of all the beatings you took.

So yeah, of course I lied about my health before that season. All I wanted was a chance to play again, and the last thing I wanted was a knee injury to keep me out of the lineup. It was the same old thinking. Still have a headache from that fight you were in last week? Take some Tylenol and you'll be good to go. That's pretty much how we all thought. It was the ultimate macho game back then. I knew my career was winding down. But I wanted to impress management and I wanted to impress every NHL team out there, showing them that I could come back from an injury like that—from multiple injuries over the past few years, in reality—and be an effective player. That was the goal. Keep going and make the end of my NHL career a successful one. Maybe get another contract.

As fate would have it, the 1995–96 season would be my final NHL campaign. Speed was what my game was founded on, and my legs weren't quite what they had been. I was 33 and coming off ACL surgery. How could my legs possibly be quite the same? Plus, the game was starting to change, as it does in every generation. Guys were getting bigger and faster. They were getting better.

Even though expansion had probably diluted the playing field a bit, you could see the difference.

Making matters worse, it was an unreal shitshow in Ottawa. Rick Bowness got fired and replaced by Dave Allison. Then Allison got fired and got replaced by Jacques Martin, who would be a Penguins assistant coach a generation later. It's one thing to play for a bad team, but three head coaches in one year? Come on. People were getting fired left and right during that time. Randy Sexton, whom I have a lot of respect for—he'd work for the Penguins in the future—got fired. The only thing that kept me sane was a young assistant general manager in Ottawa by the name of Ray Shero. Boy, was I impressed with him from the very beginning. It's no surprise to me that Ray has been such a successful general manager, winning the Cup with the Penguins in 2009. You could see back then that he was an incredibly sharp guy. He was real pro, too. And I guess you could say he learned the hard way how to run an NHL team, because there were serious issues in Ottawa back then.

My time in Ottawa wasn't all bad, mind you. I enjoyed some of my coaches there, and I liked some of my teammates. And if you've never been there, you should give it a try. It's an absolutely beautiful city. Downtown Ottawa is a breathtaking place. Unfortunately, where the Senators play is a lengthy drive south of the city. But it's not a bad place, and I'd never put it down. It was just a really, really awful place to play during this point in time, especially after the highs I had experienced. Of course, I wasn't there for long.

I played in 13 games for the Senators that season, tallying my final NHL goal. When I broke into the league a decade earlier in Pittsburgh, I probably never imagined that my NHL career would end with a whimper like that, playing on a bum knee for a lowly expansion team. Some things, though, can't be controlled. In the grand scheme of things, I was hardly ashamed of anything. I won the Stanley Cup twice with an all-time great hockey team. I made a few million dollars. I played in 477 NHL games. I scored 88 goals. I played defense and forward at the NHL level. I came back from a life-threatening fall to play again. I came back from a torn ACL to play again. I scored 13 playoff goals in 56 career postseason games. I played in 10 Stanley Cup playoff series—all with the Penguins—and we won nine of them. I'd never have imagined that June 1, 1992, in Chicago would be the last time I ever played in an NHL postseason game, but still, I have no regrets. For a kid who wasn't drafted, I did a lot of things in my NHL career and, honestly, I knew I wasn't very good anymore. In my own way, I had made peace with the fact that my NHL career was about over.

My hockey career, however, had a few chapters left. Oh, the Senators didn't want me anymore, but there were different procedures in place back in those days. So, what happened next? I got loaned to the Detroit Vapors of the IHL.

And you know what? It was an awesome experience for me. No, it wasn't the NHL, but it was still hockey and it was a totally first-class operation. Brad Shaw was there, too. He was making $450,000 a year and I was still making $500,000. The whole thing was a bit of a gong show, but not in a bad way. The Vipers played at the old Palace at Auburn Hills, home of the Detroit Pistons. It was a good ways north of Detroit, but I didn't mind. I'm telling you, everything about this team was classy. It was a treat to play for them. Rick Dudley was the coach at the time. I love Rick. Talk about a hockey genius. He was really ahead of his time in some ways and just thought about the game in a totally different way than most people. I really appreciated many things about him. Of course, the only problem with Rick was that, well, he was also completely out of his mind.

But I'll tell you what: I was having fun. A lot of fun. I made an interesting decision early on during my time in Detroit. I told the coaching staff that, if needed, I was perfectly okay playing defense. It was the position where I started my hockey career and, I figured, if this was the end, I might as well finish my career on the blue line. There weren't many good defensemen on that team, but they had some talented forwards. I just figured it made more sense for me to play defense.

Holy shit, was it fun. Some of the most fun I've ever had playing the game, truth be told. There was a carefree sense to that team, to that league, and to the way I was playing the game. I was finally starting to feel better following the ACL injury, and I was just winging it. I was playing defense, but I was concentrating plenty on the offensive side of things. I was making these end-to-end rushes, just skating all over the place. There was something very liberating and refreshing about it. It was quite a workout, too. We didn't have a lot of great defensemen on that team, so I was pretty much playing 25 minutes a night. I didn't care. I was actually kind of enjoying it. I think my mindset was, *You're probably done, so just go out there and be yourself.*

By the spring of 1996, I was feeling pretty good. My knee was better and, even though I was out of the only league I'd ever wanted to play in, my spirits were pretty high. Detroit was a great hockey town and it supported the Vipers pretty well. Playing there was a totally cool experience. Given that I had a good season in Detroit and proved I was still versatile enough to play two separate positions, I started dreaming about the NHL again. Why the hell not, right? One more contract. One more run at the Cup. Taking the ice one more time in front of a crowd of almost 20,000 hockey fans. Yeah, it's a hell of a drug, playing in the NHL. You never lose that excitement you feel when you play the game in that league. You never forget it and you always want it back. I figured I wasn't too old for the league and that my knee was finally healthy.

But it just wasn't meant to be. That summer, sadly, I didn't hear from any NHL teams. The Penguins were doing everything in their power to keep their core together. Their finances weren't good at all but Mario, Jagr, and the rest of the big boys still needed to be paid. I know Craig always appreciated the way I played the game, but I truly believe his hands were tied with the financial restrictions. That was disappointing, obviously.

Another guy from my past, though, gave me a call and wanted me to continue with my hockey career.

CHAPTER 18
SEEING
THE WORLD

While I was disappointed I didn't get an NHL contract that summer, I wasn't really shocked. I could kind of see the writing on the wall for a while.

I did, however, get a call from an old friend, Gene Ubriaco. He offered me a contract with the Chicago Wolves in the IHL. Some guys didn't like Gene and his way of coaching, but he and I loved each other from Day 1. I was always his guy, and I loved it. Plus, Chicago was my kind of town. Then there was the reality that teams weren't exactly knocking down my door with contract offers. How could I say no?

That was an interesting summer. I always wanted to buy a big RV, so that summer, I did it. That baby was 44 feet and, if I may say so, it was luxurious. I always wanted to get one and drive it cross country, which is what I did. My brother and I drove from New Hampshire, where I bought it, to Los Angeles. We had a great time.

I was single again and enjoying my life. The RV was an added bonus. My brother and I were having a blast in California. That's when I got the call from Ubriaco. It was about time to get serious because the season wasn't far away. So, it was in my best interest to make my way to Chicago immediately. I figured it was wise to drive my brother back with me to Chicago, then put him on a plane from Chicago to Boston. So that's what we did.

When I showed up for training camp at Allstate Arena, I still had my RV, naturally. On the first day of camp, a couple of workers at the arena were checking out this beauty of an RV. One of them said, "We'll just plug you in, and you can keep it here."

What a perfect idea. It had it all. Big satellite TV, the works. So, I stayed there during all of training camp and, even though it wasn't the NHL, I didn't mind it. I was still a professional hockey player.

As the season began, I really struggled to find an apartment that satisfied me. The problem was, no matter how many apartments or houses I checked out, none of them compared to this damn RV. I'm telling you, it was that great. So, I just lived in the RV all season. I met a guy who lived in a really nice mobile home. I'm not talking about trailer parks. This thing was nice. I ended up moving in right beside him and, quite honestly, it was the most fun I had in quite some time.

You must understand, Chicago is one hell of a fun town. It's probably my favorite road city. Plus, I was a newly single guy.

As the season elapsed, however, I wasn't having fun. I got two really bad concussions that season, in fact, and they weren't by accident. See, in the IHL, there were a lot of good hockey players, but most of them weren't particularly well known. I had two Stanley Cup rings and played in the league for a decade, though. Maybe I wasn't on billboards throughout Chicago, but you had damn well better believe that players in the league knew precisely who I was. And because they had heard of me, they were taking runs at me time and time again. It was awful. If you were an NHL guy with Cups, that's all it took. You had a big bullseye on your back at all times. In that regard, it was kind of a throwback with a Wild West feel. It was pretty unsettling. Plus, I'd been through hell in recent years. The fall off the mountain. The blown ACL. I was in my mid-thirties at this point. Now I'm getting multiple concussions in a season, and God knows how many I'd had in my career already.

Following that season, I realized it was time for a change. Hello, Germany.

I've always had a fondness for traveling and I wasn't afraid to play in Europe, even if it did mean a culture change. I ended up signing with a team just south of Munich and, I must say, playing in Germany was a truly great experience. I still remember stepping off the plane. It just felt good.

When you played for a team in Germany back then, you were treated well. They gave you an apartment and a brand-new car. The cars they gave you were fine, but nothing special. I've always had a sweet tooth for the good life, and boy did I get lucky. Over there, it wasn't about making money at the gate. You're playing in front of 2,500 people a night, so that's not where the money was for ownership. Nah, over there, it's all about sponsor money. It just so happens that one of our sponsors owned a Mercedes dealership. Oh, hell yes. This guy was a big hockey fan. And he loved my Stanley Cup rings. Adored them.

So he took me to his dealership. Showed me a black two-seater convertible. I told him it was the most beautiful car I'd ever seen. I wasn't lying.

He brought me back to his office. He said, "Let's do a lease." I'm thinking it's going to cost me a fortune to lease a car like that. He asked which car I liked, and I almost started laughing. He knew which one I liked. Then he told me to write down a number. I'm thinking to myself, *I really don't want to insult this guy with a low offer, but I don't want to pay a fortune for it, either.*

I wrote down 750 DM. Then I got nervous. That's not much money per month for a 100,000 DM car. He pushed it back to me and said, "Write down another number." Uh oh. Did I piss him off? Or was he being nice? I could tell he was being nice. So I wrote down 500 DM. Which, by the way, was about the equivalent of $300 U.S. at the time. I'll never forget it. He responded, "Good for you? Good for me." So, for a year, I enjoyed driving the most beautiful car I had ever seen. Being a hockey player has its perks, and I enjoyed every damn one of them.

The next season, I did the German thing again. It wasn't so bad. The seasons were only 52 games, so your body felt a hell of a lot better. The hockey was still at a pretty high level and games over there weren't nearly as violent. It was almost like a nice early retirement. I was still being paid fairly well, and for those two years in Germany, I can honestly say I was happy. I was kind of getting my emotional state back in order while still playing the game I loved.

Now that I think about it, though, that car was only the second-most beautiful thing I ever saw in Germany. Allow me to tell you about Angela.

I went to play in Hamburg the next season. It was great. And so was Angela.

About a month into the season, my German teammates started telling me about the saunas in Germany. They were telling me these saunas were co-ed, and typically enjoyed nude. Which meant they presented a wonderful opportunity to meet beautiful naked women. Just a second. Hold on. This can't be real life. I didn't believe this at first. No way. I realized that European culture was a little more...open to the fun life. But this sounded like total bullshit to me.

Me being me, I went to one of the saunas I was told about. I had to check it out. I had talked with some buddies back in the States, and they demanded that I check these places out to see if it was the real thing. It didn't take much convincing.

So, I found a place. I got a good workout in. I was on my good behavior, too. I wasn't being a creep, just enjoying a nice workout. But then I saw Angela. She was from Romania but was living in Germany. She had olive skin and jet-black hair. And what a body. It was insane. I thought to myself, *Well, I'd like to see her naked in the sauna, but I'm sure that's not going to happen.*

After I worked out, I hit the sauna. All I saw at first were two naked guys. Shit. But they were good for some information, at least. One guy told me, "It's true. There are naked women in here all the time."

So, this was good news. Apparently it wasn't a myth. I couldn't wait to tell my buddies. At this point, I was bound and determined to see some naked women. I stayed in the sauna for a few minutes. And then a few more minutes. I was getting pretty warm. Then I got hot. I don't know how long I was in there, but it felt like hours. It was probably to the point of being unsafe. But my mindset at the time was, *Fuck it. I'm going to wait until I see a naked woman.*

And then, there she was.

The door opened, and in walked Angela. Now, I'm nothing if not a gentleman, so I felt it only appropriate that I slide over to her direction and begin a conversation. One problem, though. She didn't speak a damn word of English. Thankfully, my new German pals were still around, so I had them act as translators and ask her out on a date for me.

It started out a little bumpy. We had coffee at the fitness center. She barely spoke English and I barely spoke German—or Romanian—so it was kind of rough. Then, I totally freaked her out, although through no fault of my own. She thought I followed her home from the coffee shop. She thought I was stalking her, basically. And she freaked out.

This wasn't the case, though. It turns out that she literally lived a block away from me. Once she understood this, she relaxed. Two weeks later, she was moving her stuff into my place. Yeah, there was serious chemistry there, English or no English. For the first three months of our relationship, we didn't go anywhere without a German-English dictionary. But we ended up dating for two years and, I have to say, she was a very special woman. And not just in the looks department. She was awesome.

Angela and I weren't meant to be, though. Logistics got in the way. I loved my couple of years in Germany, but it was time for me to get back home to the United States. My career was over, and I knew it. It was time for me to move on with my life. I would have brought Angela back home with me. I wanted to. But she wasn't ready for that. She had a life in Germany and didn't want to be too far away from her family. I totally understood, even though I was going to miss her. She was a great girl, and I have nothing but fond memories when I think of her. But it was time to come home and to move on with my life.

CHAPTER 19
A NEW LIFE

It was the early 2000s. My career was over and I was living back in Boston. I felt like my next career would probably be in media and, naturally, I wanted to be involved with the Penguins. By this point, I had been gone for eight years, which was quite hard to believe. But I figured being around the Penguins was the best thing for me. Mario now owned the team. I still knew a lot of people in Pittsburgh. And when you've won championships in a city—especially in a sports town like the 'Burgh—people still know you, too.

Mike Lange and Paul Steigerwald were doing TV broadcasts in Pittsburgh, as they had for quite some time. Some changes were ultimately coming, though. They moved Steigy to the radio side to do play-by-play. This meant a spot was open on TV for the color commentary position. I was probably never going to be a play-by-play guy, as I'd never been trained for it. Doing color commentary, though, is different. I realized that most teams had employed former players for that role. The community knows who we are, and we know the game. It all kind of makes sense.

I found myself getting an interview with Fox Sports Net for the TV job alongside Mike, whom I had always loved. I had a lawyer in Pittsburgh join me for the interview and, to be honest, I felt pretty good about the entire process. I was told they'd be in touch, and that was that. But then two weeks went by. And then a third. You know how it is. When that much time elapses, chances are things aren't going to end well. And that was the case.

Later, I found out that my old roommate in New York, Edzo, got the job. Hell, I couldn't be upset with that. Not at all. He already had a bit of experience on broadcasts. He was smooth. He was likable. He was personable. He played a couple of years in Pittsburgh, so the fans knew who he was. I totally understood. I wasn't insulted in the least. And you know what? A part of me was a little relieved.

The truth is, I absolutely wanted to take a year off to do whatever the hell I wanted. So, what did I do?

I went bungee jumping in British Columbia. I went skydiving in New Hampshire. I bought a Harley and drove it everywhere. I rented a car and drove all through Western Europe.

I just needed it. I was always a man of adventure. Seeing the world is important if you have the opportunity, and that's exactly what I had. Don't get me wrong, the life of a professional hockey player is a great thing. You'll never hear me complain about it. But it does take a physical toll on your body and on your mind. I felt like I needed that year off. I was single, didn't have any kids and didn't have a job. But I had money in the bank. So, I enjoyed all that life had to offer that year.

But me being me, perhaps I enjoyed it a little too much. After that year, I looked at my bank account. And I did a bit of a double take. *Oh, shit.* Hockey had been great to me. I had made around $3 million. But I had a habit of living the life. Plus, I was bent over badly in my divorce settlement. I had too much money going out and not enough coming in. It was time to go back to work.

I tried to dabble in sales a little, but I didn't like it that much. It didn't really work out for me. Suddenly, I didn't know what to do. And I entered another rough phase in my life. It seems I'm always on a bit of a roller coaster, from happiness to sadness, then back again. Getting invited to camp and becoming a pro was so great, but then there was some depression because it took me so long to finally establish myself in the NHL. Then I finally reached the pinnacle of my career, winning the Cup twice and being rewarded with a rich contract. But then came the accident, the injuries, and the end of my NHL career. Germany and that year off revived me.

And now? Now, I was out of work and starting to lose money. It's a pretty damn stressful feeling if you've ever been there. I ultimately went three years without a steady job. Remember how I used to feel nervous before games, how that anxiety could be a problem for me? I was starting to get nervous about my life and how I was going to manage things. I was really nervous.

I felt like I was at a crossroads. Something needed to give. I had called Craig Patrick asking if there were scouting jobs or anything else available with the Penguins. He said he didn't have any openings. I had exhausted every avenue. In the end, I called the big guy. Mario, I figured, would have the answer. It's not just that he was the owner of the team, though that didn't hurt. It was just that he was...Mario.

"Let's have lunch," Mario said. "Meet me at the golf course."

We met at Nevillewood, and I poured my heart out to him. I remember telling him, "I need a job. I need help."

Mario stayed nice and calm, just like always. He offered me some advice along the way. "I need you to get back to Pittsburgh," he said. "Start networking. Get your name out there. And I will help you."

So, I listened to Mario. During the 2002–03 season, Mario was still playing. Hell, he led the league in scoring by 20 points halfway through the season before injuries finally caught up to him. But he wasn't just the greatest hockey player ever. He was a good businessman and a friend. So, I kept on listening to his advice in my head. I was going back and forth from Boston to Pittsburgh a ton during this season. I'm doing radio hits on WDVE in Pittsburgh. I was doing a show called *Inside Penguins Hockey*. I did what Mario wanted me to do. I got my name back out there. I started making the rounds. I started to catch up with old friends and make some new ones. I wasn't really making any money doing this, but I was laying the foundation that Mario thought I needed.

Along the way, I was enjoying myself. The Penguins weren't very good at this point. Jagr became too expensive and had been traded a couple of years earlier. Alex Kovalev, one of the most talented hockey players I've ever seen, was traded during this season. The Penguins couldn't really afford to keep him anymore. Mario was still pretty new at being an owner, and he was doing a great job, but he knew that certain expenses had to be cut. Remember, this was pre-lockout, pre-salary cap, pre-new arena. Mario knew exactly what he was doing and he was still a draw, of course, so people would still come see him play. The Penguins were building for the future, and I was hoping to be a part of that on some level. I could see what they were doing, and I was damn happy to be spending more days in Pittsburgh. It felt good. It felt right.

Then, it happened.

In May 2003, I got a call from Mario.

"Hey, Bourquey," he said. "I want you to come to Mellon Arena tomorrow. You need to talk with [Penguins Vice President of Communications] Tom McMillan. We've got something for you. We'd like to offer you the radio position. Are you interested?"

At the time, I didn't really have a clue what was going on. The whole thing felt like kind of a mystery to me. But I wasn't complaining, and I wasn't about to turn down the offer. It's what I had been waiting for. As it turns out, the Penguins were making a rather unorthodox move. Craig was still the general manager at this time, and he decided to make a coaching change. Edzo was about to become the head coach, even though he didn't really have any coaching experience. It didn't totally shock me, though. Edzo is a very intelligent, charismatic man. He had the right personality for coaching, and the team wasn't very good, so maybe they'd be patient with him. His departure, of course, left a vacancy in the TV booth. The team decided to move Bob Errey from radio to TV.

At that point in time, I was in so much trouble. I didn't have a regular income. I didn't have a whole lot of confidence. I had no idea what I was getting into next. This was the opportunity I was waiting for, and I wasn't about to blow it.

Some things haven't changed from the '80s until now. If you talk with players in the league right now and ask them what they'd be doing for a living if they weren't professional hockey players, I'm willing to bet about 90 percent of them would have zero fucking idea. Zero. It's what you do your whole life, this game. From the time you're a kid, you're trained to eat, breathe, and sleep hockey and not much else. You get up at 4:00 AM for practices. You get extra ice time when you can. You watch videos to make yourself better and to understand team concepts better. You watch your diet. You educate yourself on the game in every way possible. Hockey. Hockey. Hockey. For most of us, there never was a Plan B or a Plan C. You either made it, or you had a life of shit.

I made it, all right. But I didn't have $20 million in the bank when I was done. Was a lot of that my fault? Sure, it was. I should have watched my money more. I should have done a lot of things better. But it wasn't all in my control. Hockey was really all I knew, which is why I'm so fortunate that Mario called me that day.

You become accustomed to a certain lifestyle when you play in the NHL. You've got to have the nicest car, the nicest house, the nicest clothes. I was dishing out money left and right. What I wasn't dishing out, Julie was spending on her own. The habit I had of always picking up every check at dinner never went away. It was always there. It's kind of an addiction, you might say. When my career was over, I was finally able to come to grips with this and I found some peace in wanting an everyday job, a somewhat settled life. Still, that's not so easy. I needed to get my foot in the door somehow.

Thank God for Mario. It all goes back to him. Look at the team over the years, the media, the coaching staff. The bond that we had in 1991 and 1992 never goes away.

I've been involved in broadcasting. Bob Errey and Peter Taglianetti, too. Troy Loney has done media ventures with the Penguins, as has Kenny Wregget. Bryan Trottier has been an assistant coach. Same with Joey Mullen, Mark Recchi, and Rick Tocchet. Kevin Stevens has had numerous stints as a scout. Who does the intermission reports on TV? Jay Caufield, naturally. We were the team that made hockey in Pittsburgh a big deal. The bond we had will never be broken. Maybe we were a bunch of renegades, a bunch of cowboys, a bunch of hard-headed alpha males. But we always loved each other too, and as the years pass, I can't tell you how nice it is to have all of these guys involved on the same team again during different eras.

It took a decade, and there were plenty of low moments in that decade.

But I was back in Pittsburgh, a part of the Penguins again. It's funny how happy I started to feel once this deal was signed. Being a part of the Penguins was something I truly needed. I was home.

CHAPTER 20
HAPPILY EVER AFTER

The last 16 years have been some of the best in my life. Going to work every day is a true blessing because I find myself in the broadcast booth with the amazing Mike Lange. The Hall of Famer. The legend.

Mikey is 70 now, not a kid. He's lived the life, live hard, work hard, play hard. I hope he lives forever, even though I know he won't. There are a lot of things about my relationship with Mike that are hard to ignore. Is he family? You bet your ass he is. I love that man so much. I care about him. I like seeing him smile. But our relationship is even deeper than that.

It's a two-way street with Mikey and me. So many people know him as the voice of the Pittsburgh Penguins, and make no mistake, he will always be the voice of the Penguins. Not many other people, however, truly know him. Mike has a very, very small inner circle. Not many people are allowed inside of said circle. So, to not only be embraced by him on a professional level, but also on a personal level, is one of the most special things that's ever happened to me. I truly mean that. There's a part of me that loves coming to work every day just so I can see him.

Of course, there's also the part of me that realizes Mike isn't going to be around for 20 or 30 more years. The chances of that are pretty slim, I realize. So, there is this part of me that wants to be with him all the time, because I cherish those moments with him. I consider it a true honor to be as close to him as I am. He's a good man and much more than just the play-by-play guy with all the funny sayings. I like to think I know him as well as anyone ever has. And believe me, it's not easy. Mikey is so private. He's so reserved. He's a lone wolf who likes to howl at the moon all by himself on most occasions. And I respect that, as I respect him. But when I get the call to go howl at the moon with the Hall of Famer, you'd better believe I say yes.

My relationship with Mike was always good when I played, but it wasn't what it is now, of course. It wasn't uncommon at that time for the broadcasters to have a beer or two with the players on the road. Things are different now. The players don't really drink anymore, and if they do, it certainly isn't with the broadcasters or the fans. It was a different world when I played. Mikey hasn't changed all that much, though. I suppose he has slowed down a bit, but he still loves the game, still loves the city. He's just got a presence about him that's a little different. My relationship with him has so much depth. It brings me joy on a daily basis.

I'm going to have to accept the fact that Mike is going to retire at some point. I realize this. But I'm not ready for that day, and I'm pretty sure Penguins fans aren't ready for that day. And you know what? Mike isn't, either. Not yet. I tell him all the time that he can't even be thinking about retirement, that it's too soon, that too many seasons remain. He just rolls his eyes at me and says, "Okay, Bourquey." But I know damn well that he still likes to hear it. Being the voice of the Pittsburgh Penguins is why he wakes up every morning. It's what drives him. It's what gets his body moving. It's what gets his head moving. It's what gets his heart moving. I truly believe it's his one passion in life, being Mike Lange, voice of the Pittsburgh Penguins. He loves his blues music. But other than that, it's just the Penguins. He's still so motivated to be the very best in the business every single night. And to me, he still is.

I think it's fair to say that he enjoys being Mike Lange. Penguins practices are generally open to the public in Cranberry Township. You should see it when he's at practice. The guy gets surrounded like he's a member of The Beatles. And in Pittsburgh, make no mistake, he is that big. He loves it. On the surface, he comes across as being so very humble about his celebrity and his importance to the city. But deep down, I'm telling you, he loves it. He absolutely loves it. When he feels all the love and admiration from Penguins fans, that's his sweet spot. You can feel it. He's absolutely at his happiest when he's around the game, around the Penguins, around the fans who have adored him for generations. Mario is the most important and most popular person in franchise history and always will be. I'm not so sure Mike Lange isn't No. 2 on the list. He's that big of a deal to the franchise. Pittsburgh has been lucky to showcase many broadcasting legends, guys like Bob Prince and Myron Cope. Mikey obviously deserves to be in their class. And really, to me, he's in a class of his own.

I'll tell you what my favorite thing about Mike, in terms of being a professional, truly is. It's his work ethic. I think there's a perception out there that guys like Mike just show up at the rink and sit behind a microphone for three hours, that it's really that easy. Boy, is that wrong.

Luckily, I don't mind a little bit of hard work, and given my profession, it's a good thing. To be honest, I kind of enjoy hard work. I've always been like that. I was a bricklayer's assistant. I worked in construction. Blacktop crew. Yeah, I like hard work. It's part of who I am. It's probably the one good thing that my dad taught me. But here's the thing: when I started broadcasting games, I thought I'd be so good at it without any preparation. I didn't even consider that it was a big part of the job. In my mind, I'm thinking, *I played professional hockey for 18 years. This is a piece of cake. I'll just slide into the booth and talk. It will be great.*

Then, I listened to my first couple of games. I immediately thought to myself, *Man, this doesn't sound so good. Not at all.*

Then I started watching other broadcasters and how they went about their business. In particular, I started watching Mike. I knew he was a legend and I already had so much respect for him. But the level of my respect only grew when I started studying him daily. It was artistry and hard work merged into one. Mike always has these stats prepared for every game, but most of them he doesn't even use on the air. He doesn't want to show off and randomly throw them out there during broadcasts. Instead, he waits for the right moment and, if it presents itself, Mike will throw a number or two out there. Little stuff like that. The tidbits he has and the backstories he takes the time to know, it's really incredible. So many of the stories don't get told, but some do. Holy cow, did all this make me smarter. It made me better at the job. I basically started emulating him and, hell, if you're going to emulate anyone in this business, why not him? I've changed so very much over the years as a broadcaster. I take my notes before every game. I take it very, very seriously. The homework I do is pretty intense, pretty thorough. I'm just trying to keep up with the Hall of Famer, after all. It's made me a better broadcaster, a more prepared hockey mind. Sure, I know the game. I've always known the game and, hey, having played in the league for as long as I did obviously has its advantages. I learned that it takes a lot more than that, however. I feel like my broadcasting has evolved and improved a lot over the years, and I credit the man who sits to my left with so much of that. He absolutely showed me the way.

Being a broadcaster is a funny thing, though. I'm a big believer that you can still cheer for a team but be objective. When the Penguins score a big goal, I've got a little dance I do. I'm a Penguin through and through. Just because I'm a team employee, though, doesn't mean that I'm not going to call it how I see it. There are people in my position around the league who refuse to bite the hand that feeds them. They'll never criticize their team. Not me.

Trust me, I'm aware of it. Mikey, not so much. He doesn't bother with that as much. He lets me do that stuff, like taking a member of the Penguins to task if it's deserved. And listen, sometimes it is. I'm aware of how great they've been during the past dozen years. Three Cups, four appearances in the Final. That's a special thing, to say the least, and I've had the honor to broadcast some of the greatest players to play the game. Sid. Geno. And so many others. But does that mean the Penguins are beyond criticism? Of course it doesn't, and I couldn't do my job any other way. I call it as I see it, which means, from time to time, I'll call out a member of the Penguins.

Sometimes I probably go a little too far. I admit it. I drive home some nights and a cringe a little bit. Sometimes I go overboard, no doubt. But a few things go into this. I feel like I need to be honest. I respect the Pittsburgh Penguins; I respect the guys in that sweater, and I respect the educated hockey fans who are listening to our broadcasts. So, you know what? I'm not going to lie. I tell it like it is. If I were a player and a former player were analyzing me on a broadcast, I wouldn't want to get destroyed, but I'd want him to tell the truth. So that's why I do what I do.

At the same time, I keep something else in mind. Somewhere out there, this guy has a family and they may be listening. A mom. A dad. A wife. A girlfriend. A son. A daughter. A grandpa. A grandma. An aunt. An uncle. A brother. A sister.

Thus, I'm always going to be respectful. I've been there. Also, you have to walk into the locker room in my line of work, and quite often. It's very important for myself and Mikey to have a great relationship with these guys. Very important. You get to know guys, get to understand why they did certain things during games, stuff like that. It's all part of my job. Plus, the fact of the matter is, people in my line of work spend more time at the rink and with players than we do with our families. That's reality. So, you better get along with those people and not cross any lines if you want to have professional and personal relationships. Do I walk a tight rope? Yeah, of course I do. I admit it. But I'll say this: I've been

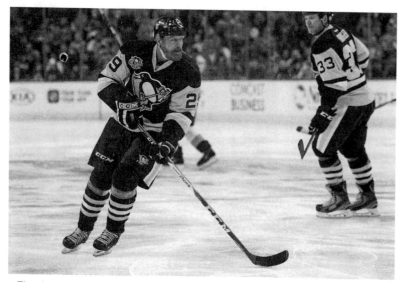

The alumni game is a special way to get back on the ice in the Black and Gold. (AP Images)

broadcasting Penguins games for 15 years. Never, not one time, has a player confronted me about anything I've said on the air. Likewise, never, not one time, has anyone from the Pittsburgh Penguins told me to tone down my style. They have always, always trusted me to walk the line, and I can't tell you how much that means to me. It's just me being me.

My broadcasting career triggered a more settled, satisfying time in my life. I believe life goes in 10-year cycles. Think about your life in terms of each decade. That's what I do, anyway. And I think it's real. A new cycle had arrived for me with broadcasting. And not long after, my children were born. Being a dad—and a better dad than my father was—was always a dream of mine. It finally happened on June 23, 2004, when Madison was born.

There was a problem, though. It became clear not long after she was born that Madison was deaf. What a scary feeling as a parent.

219

In fact, Madison was born profoundly deaf in both ears. She had her first cochlear implants to attempt to cure her deafness when she was one. At two, she had her second. Through the miracle that is modern science, Madison can hear today. She went to the Western Pennsylvania School for the Deaf for years, but then she was mainstreamed into elementary school. She's in high school now, and she's a distinguished honor student. How about that? I'm so, so proud of her. And she already knows what she wants to do for a living. She still has memories of the anesthesiologists who helped her when she was two years old. Can you believe that? Ever since then, it's what she's wanted to do for a living. It was so scary to know something was wrong with my first child, my only daughter. To know she's okay now? And that her future is so bright? It's a special thing.

Dylan was born on March 24, 2006. The little Two-Niner, as some like to call him. Dylan isn't quite the rebel his old man was—and he's a lot smarter—but when I look at him, I absolutely see myself. He's all boy and just a great kid. He's a talented athlete, too. He looks like an athlete. He's built like an athlete. He's a goalie in hockey and a catcher in baseball.

It's quite a thrill for me to watch him play hockey, as you can imagine. The feeling of pride I get when I watch him take the ice isn't easy for me to put into words. But it's a powerful thing.

The fact of the matter is, I have very much lived the life. I lived the life that people dream of when they think about being a professional athlete. I worked my ass off through the ranks. I finally made it. I made a lot of money. I won championships. I had more women than I can remember, and they were all beautiful. It all sounds so incredible, I know. Some of it really was. But you don't find true fulfillment in your life until all your dreams come true, and having children was more important to me than any of those other things.

The Stanley Cup parade is just as special from the other side of the broadcast. (Getty Images)

I feel like so many things in our lives are already laid out. Decisions that we make go north and south, and there are consequences. For the most part, despite my wild side, I believe I've taken the right roads. When I haven't, I've dealt with consequences. Things have gotten bumpy. I've gone off-roading. But I've never ended up in a ditch. Through it all, I've been honest about it. I've been me. And nothing has come easily for me, I assure you. Not the hockey career, not the broadcasting career, none of it. I worked for everything I ever had, which is why I think the people of Pittsburgh and I have always had a good relationship. Have I taken advantage of opportunities? Of course I have. But I've never taken the easy path to anything and, in my experience, Pittsburgh can sniff that out in a heartbeat. Those who have taken the easy road are never quite respected here. It's not how this city operates. While I may be a proud son of Boston, I can truly tell you that Pittsburgh is my home. Even when I was away for years, it was always on my mind, always where I felt the most comfortable.

I suppose there are parallels between that mindset and the Penguins. For the past 15-plus years, I have had the same routine. I wake up and head to the rink, visit practices and morning skates, and broadcast games, and everything else that comes with it. This isn't an ordinary organization, nor has it been an ordinary life. I suppose it's fitting. Sometimes while I'm broadcasting, I will call the team the Penguinees. What's a Penguinee, you ask? It's a team that does things its own way. A team that will fall 3–0 then roar back from behind to win. A team that will protect a one-goal lead in the third period by trying to score more. A team others are jealous of because of its talent but that, when you look deep into the players' hearts, you see they're working harder than anyone else. It's a franchise that's been bankrupt—twice—but that has always experienced great riches.

I admit I see some parallels. I've been to the top of the mountain. I've been to the damn bottom of that mountain, too. My life almost ended at the bottom of a mountain, but since then, I've climbed my way back up. Just like the Penguinees.

It's funny how you have certain snapshots in your mind that never go away, that shape your life. I still think of that moment when I chose Kingston over college hockey, when I chose Pittsburgh over Boston, when I lifted the Cup those two times, when I laid at the bottom of a mountain, when I decided to come home from Germany, when I was in serious trouble and called Mario, when my children were born, and when I was proudly able to broadcast three more championship teams. What a life.

When the Penguins won the Cup in Nashville in 2017, I had some postgame work to do. It was a blur, but a blast, as the Penguins won 2–0 to clinch the Cup.

The gang back together at the Winter Classic alumni game. (Getty Images)

About an hour after the game, Mikey was kind of enjoying a quiet moment to himself. He was thinking about his career, about all the magic he had witnessed. I left him alone in his thoughts for a little bit. He deserved that moment and, really, it was perfect. He's such a loner in his own way, I wanted him to have those quiet moments to himself to absorb it all. He was in Music City, and he's a music man if ever there's been one. What a city for Mikey to call a Stanley Cup Final in, even if we were all quietly hoping that this would be the time the Penguins would win a Cup at home.

Me? I'm no introvert. So I made my way downstairs and headed for one more locker room celebration. There once was a time that I'd race into the locker room head-first, double-fisting, ready for the party. I went a little slower this time, but my head was held high.

I wouldn't want to be a part of any other organization. I'm a Pittsburgh Penguin for life. To win two Cups as a player and to be a bridge between the greatest fans in the world and the squad in my second run with the franchise has truly been a dream.

I wasn't born with a silver spoon in my mouth, and neither were the Pittsburgh Penguins. My dad used to kick the shit out of me when I had a bad hockey game, just like the Patrick Division used to kick the shit out of the Penguins for so long. Then, one day, the Penguins grew up. I'm happy to say I did, too.

The Penguins are still going strong in 2019, and so am I. What a thrill it's been. It took me quite a while to get here, but I'm a happy man.

CHAPTER 21
DREAM TEAM(MATES)

Along the way, it occurred to me that I couldn't write a book about my years with the Pittsburgh Penguins without singling out a few of my teammates. I loved every damn one of them, but there are a few guys who deserve a special mention.

When you look at the Penguins of the early '90s, the first thing you notice is the pure talent, right? And I'm not denying that. We played with the greatest player of all time, and he was hardly the only Hall of Famer. It was a goddamn Hall of Fame wing, really. But the talent you saw watching on TV or at the Igloo was only part of what made that team special. I'm telling you, the heart and the character—and the carefree nature—of these guys was very much part of what made us a special hockey team and a special group of people.

You don't win championships on talent alone, and I don't give a shit if that's a cliché. You just don't. You have to be a family, a bunch of brothers. You simply have to be. If you don't have that, you don't really have anything at all. That's exactly what we were. No one really fought. We bickered all the time, like families always do. But there was a real love there, a real bond. When I think back to those days, I think about the friendships even more than I think about those two magical springs in 1991 and 1992. These are a few of the guys who really stick out in my memory.

John Cullen

I'll love John Cullen until the day I die. I hate that he never got his name on the Stanley Cup, because that man was a champion. It's funny; on the magical night in Minnesota when we won the Stanley Cup, I think I thought about Johnny more than I thought about my teammates. I mean that. We don't win that Cup without what we did in the regular season. And more than that—what a warrior, what a guy.

In 1988, he fought Mike Keane in the Montreal Forum. To this day, it was the greatest fight I've ever seen. I've never seen two guys throw punches with more might. It was a hell of a thing to see. Johnny was probably 5'9", but he played and presented himself like he was 6'5". He had some of the best hands of anybody I played with. He really did. What an unreal hockey player he was. He's battled health issues in his life and he wasn't even drafted, and look at what he made of himself. When I think of people in the game who I have a lot of respect for, I can assure you John Cullen is right at the very top. He lived hard, he played hard. He was special, an unreal human being. I can honestly say it was an honor being that guy's teammate, and it's an honor to call him a friend.

Mark Recchi

Rex came into the NHL like gangbusters. When I started to watch him play, I realized he was going to be special. Maybe not Hall of Fame special, but special nonetheless.

We lived together for a while in Upper St. Clair and got to know each other so very well. We did everything together. We got to know each other's families so well. We pretty much became brothers, and he's still a great friend of mine to this day.

Rex always played with a chip on his shoulder and, at his size, I guess you had to. Back in the '80s, smaller players were absolutely discriminated against. No question about it. So, Rex had this intensity about him that never went away. Finally, though, you could see the softer side of him when he was away from the rink.

I'm so happy that he's back with the Penguins on the coaching staff. He's played in a lot of places, but he'll always be a Penguin to me.

Kevin Stevens

Artie has been through a lot in his life. I think we're all aware of that. Through it all, you'll never hear anyone utter a bad word about him. Not one. To know Kevin Stevens is to know a wonderful human being, the best of the best, the guy you always want on your side.

We were close partially because we both came from the Boston area. Remember, Artie was drafted by the Kings, and he was traded to the Penguins one summer when we were young. We were both playing in the same summer league in Boston. I was lining up against him before a faceoff when I looked at him and said, "You're a Penguin now, just like me."

He looked up, smiled, and said, "I can't wait."

He was just a big St. Bernard of a man. He was just so much bigger and stronger that the rest of us. I guess you could say he was a little larger than life. He was our soul. When something needed to be said, he was the one who said it.

It's been so wonderful to see him overcome his addiction demons in the last few years. We're all pulling for him. There's only one Artie.

Jaromir Jagr

People forget how raw Jagr was when he came to the Penguins in 1990. He was literally a kid. That first year was really, really hard for him because he was so homesick all the time.

But the one thing that really got him through was how much he loved being at the rink. I've never seen anything quite like it. Every day Jagr came to the rink was Christmas morning for him. I don't know if that speaks volumes on where he came from at that time, or maybe he was just in love with the game that much. It was something to see.

Jags loved the attention. We had these little mailboxes back then. You know what was in his mailbox every morning when he showed up for work? KIT KAT bars and women's panties. He was asked one time what he loved about Pittsburgh, and he said, "KIT KAT bars and all of the pretty girls." So, there you have it. I was only his teammate when he was a kid, but it was nice having him around, and I don't know that we would have won those championships without him. He gave us a different kind of gear.

Jags just wanted to win. Yeah, he was a star, and stars like getting their points. But he just wanted to win and had this insatiable desire to take over games in third periods. And he always did. I'm still always happy on the rare occasions when I get to see him. He always has that same smile on his face because he's still always at the rink.

Rick Tocchet

This relationship was a complicated one because Rick came to us in the trade that sent Rex to Philadelphia. I was very upset that Rex was traded. He was my best friend on the team.

But let me tell you, I didn't mind having Rick Tocchet around. What a man. I'd have to say that he had a little bit of John Wayne in him. There was something about the way he walked, the way he shifted his weight from one side to the other. You didn't want to fuck with him, and basically, nobody did. His whole attitude toward hockey was, *If you're my teammate, you're my best friend. If you're not, there's a pretty good chance that I will kill you tonight.*

He had swagger right out of a western movie. I still remember an incident at Chicago Stadium in March 1992. A Larry Murphy shot broke his jaw, so he left the game. We all assumed he was done for a while. It was a nasty-looking injury. Then, he comes back into the game wearing this Jack Lambert–looking face guard. It wasn't a shield or a cage. It was an actual face guard. And, of course, he goes out and scores the game-winning goal, because that's the kind of guy he was—a great, great hockey player who took a lot of pride in keeping us all safe, and a hell of a man.

Mario Lemieux

I can honestly say Mario is the one person in the world who I feel awkward around. I'm in awe of him. I've been around a lot of famous people in my day, a lot of celebrities, but I've never felt in awe of them before. I feel in awe of Mario Lemieux to this day, and I probably always will.

He has a presence about him that can only be described as that of royalty. You basically feel like you're around a king when he walks into a room and, really, you kind of are. Sometimes, I'll act cool and say something like, "Hey big boy, have a good day." But really, I'm a little kid when I'm around him. It was truly an honor to play with the greatest hockey player of all time, to win championships with that guy. He led in his own way—always quiet, always cool. But he was always there for you when you needed him, on and off the ice. He never looked down at people. He was always humble, even though he knew damn well he was the greatest player who ever lived.

When you're around Mario, you know you are in the presence of greatness. How many people can you truly say that about in your lifetime? He just puts off a kind of energy that no one else has. I'm grateful to have taken the ice with him for all those years, and I'm grateful to him for being so instrumental in helping me with my second career.

Mario Lemieux is and always will be the Pittsburgh Penguins.

Bryan Trottier

Wow. What a legend, and I don't use that word lightly. Trots is someone I value very much as a friend. He was an unreal teammate and one of the great players of his time.

Think about what he did. He was already a Hall of Famer when he came to Pittsburgh, and he willingly ended up playing third fiddle to Mario and Ronnie Francis. Not even second fiddle, but third fiddle. And he did it with an amazing enthusiasm. When has a player of his stature ever happily settled for that kind of role? The man has no ego. He just has an obsession with winning the Stanley Cup, something he did twice with us and four times with the Islanders.

When Mario would be out of the lineup, Trots would wear the "C." I always sensed he felt funny about it when Bob Johnson or Scotty Bowman would ask him to wear it. He didn't want to be disrespectful to Mario. But at the same time, Trots actually felt like it was important that he did wear it, because he was carrying Mario's torch, basically. He was representing Mario when he was hurt, and he took that responsibility so seriously. I'll never forget that.

Bob Errey and Troy Loney

I'm putting these two guys together because I always think of them that way. It's funny—all three of us were role players and all three of us played left wing on those Stanley Cup teams. But there was never a rivalry between us. Sometimes Bobby had the hot hand, and when he did, he got his time with Mario. And we were happy for him. Sometimes Troy got hot, and he'd get some time with Mario or Ronnie. When that happened, hell, I was thrilled for him.

The three of us went through a lot together. We were the only three guys on the ice that night (along with Randy Hillier) in

Minnesota who were with the Penguins for a longer period of time than Mario when we won the Cup. There was a real bond there.

We were all so different. Bobby was a speedster, Troy was tough as nails, and I was some nobody defenseman from Boston. But the three of us always had a great friendship and always found a way to make everything work even though we played the same position.

They're two of the best men you'll ever meet in your life. They weren't superstars, but you win Stanley Cups with guys like Bobby and Troy.

Tom Barrasso

Some people out there don't like Tom Barrasso, and he's earned a lot of it. But I still love Tommy, and I know my teammates do, too.

When he started the Thurston Howell III shit with us, we put an end to it pretty quickly. We wouldn't allow it.

Tommy was actually a great teammate back in the '80s and early '90s. I don't know what happened to him in the later years. I know he had some disagreements with the media. But in the Cup years, he was all in, all about winning, and I always appreciated that about him.

He was always obsessed with cars—the more expensive, the better. He still is.

I wish things were different now. I hate that he holds a grudge against Pittsburgh and the Penguins. I know a lot of it stems from stuff that was said in the media, but it feels like it's a giant middle finger to all his teammates, honestly. And I hate that it has to be that way. He's always invited back to golf outings and team events, and he never shows up. I feel like he's just pushed all of us out of his life, and that's always going to upset me. I always hope he comes back one of these years. He was our goaltender, and I think we're all ready to bury all the shit that's been said if he'd come back so we could give him a hug.

Ulf Samuelsson

Jesus, what a guy. What a riverboat gambler. You know how he played, always trying to take runs at people and drive everyone nuts at all times? I'd say he lived his life that way, too. Ulfie was truly a wild man, and I loved him.

I'll never forget the 1991 playoffs. He broke his hand but didn't miss any time. He had to shake with his left hand during the handshake line at the conclusion of series.

The pain was overwhelming him before one of the games, so he had to take a painkilling shot. I had to go into the trainer's room right before a game in the Final. Ulfie was in there. I swear to God, they stuck the needle five inches into his hand. You've never heard anyone scream like that. He actually had a towel in his mouth and was just biting it as hard as he could and screaming.

But he was going to do anything in his power to play that night, and that's exactly what he did. What a warrior.

Joey Mullen

The game came so very naturally to Joey. I always felt like he was in his true element when he was sitting in the locker room. He was a rink rat, and the game of hockey made him so happy.

I can still hear that New York accent in my head. And his story is a great one. The guy played on roller skates with metal wheels in Hell's Kitchen. That's how he learned the game of hockey. And he was a pure natural. He wasn't a great skater, didn't have a booming shot, and wasn't a big guy. But you can find his bust at the Hockey Hall of Fame in Toronto. For all of you young people who never saw him play, he had a lot of Jake Guentzel in him. Always knew where to go and knew how to play with great players.

He was so smart. We all became better hockey players just talking with him, studying the things he did. He was a brilliant defensive player, a great goal scorer, just a hockey savant. He's always a kind soul, and was a proud member of the Pittsburgh Penguins.

Ron Francis

Ronnie should have been in a James Bond movie. He was that slick, that cool, that distinguished. He just had something special about him. He was maybe the most professional person I ever played with. He was always dressed perfectly, never a hair out of place. Everything about him was always just perfect.

Ronnie never misspoke, always said exactly what he wanted to articulate. He had this incredible pride about him at all times. They called him Ronnie Franchise for a reason. He was the franchise in Hartford, and what a player he was in Pittsburgh.

He always knew the rulebook better than referees. He was just a genius on and off the ice. And he was like Mario in some ways, in that he spoke exactly when it was necessary. He wasn't a chatty guy like Trots, but he was a good man and a hell of a teammate.

How many players in the history of the game rose to the occasion like he did? He scored in both of our Cup-clinching games, including the game-winner in Chicago. He played the game of his life in Game 4 in 1992 against the New York Rangers, when we needed him most. Who won the faceoff on Mario's famous goal to beat the Blackhawks in Game 1 in 1992? Ronnie, of course.

He's in the Hall of Fame for a reason. I don't know how many people on those teams you'd say were gentlemanly. A few of us, perhaps. But Ronnie was a true gentleman.

Jimmy Paek

Jimmy was the first Korean-born player to play in the NHL, and he got his name on the Cup his first two seasons in the league. And you know what? He deserved it. I loved that kid.

He would do anything to be on the ice for the Penguins, and he would have done anything to stay in Pittsburgh for 10 years. Jimmy just wanted to be part of something special. He wanted to do his part no matter what.

One of the happiest moments of my career was seeing Jimmy score against the North Stars in Game 6. The bench was so damn happy for him. He was immediately accepted and loved from Day 1.

Wendell Young

Third-string goalies don't get much in the way of love, but Wendell deserves it. He didn't play a huge role on the ice during games, but he played a huge role in every other way.

For one thing, Wendell kept us loose at all times. We had these hospitality lounges in hotels after road games in the playoffs. Wendell would get there right when games ended and set everything up. We'd have all of the food and drinks in there because of Wendell. He'd arrange for friends and family members to be there. It was incredible that he did that kind of stuff even though his job was to be a player.

He also worked incredibly hard in practice. Being a backup goalie in practice is hard work. He would stay on the ice forever with guys who wanted to get some work in. He was a special teammate and, on the rare occasion I see him, I can't wait to give him a big hug. Without question he was one of the greatest teammates I ever had.

Jay Caufield

Let's just say, Jay was a better roommate than most.

Jay was my roommate during a lot of my single years, and he saw some things that he says he'll take to his grave with him. That's probably for the best. Jay was one of the great heavyweights in the game, a tough customer if ever there has been one. Thank God he has a gentle soul.

He also worked his ass off in practice. He worked every day to make himself the best player he could be and that made a real impression on all of us.

The truth is, I could go on and on about my teammates and how special they were.

They were the best times of my life, those years with the Pittsburgh Penguins. We had it all, really. We had ownership doing its best to keep us and the city happy. We had two iconic, legendary head coaches when we needed them most. We had a bond that was surpassed only by our talent level. We had the greatest player of all time. And we had the support of a sports city that, in my opinion, has no equal.

What a time to be alive.

ACKNOWLEDGMENTS

I have learned that writing a book is a much more difficult process than I ever could have imagined. The meaning behind this book was not only to entertain but also to allow the amazing Penguins fans an opportunity to go layers deeper behind the scenes of a franchise that wallowed in mediocrity and made its way to the top of the mountain. I want to give thanks to Josh Yohe, who had the patience of Job to walk through this process with me, and the incredible staff at Triumph Books, including Bill Ames, Michelle Bruton, and Jen DePoorter. I also need to thank all my amazing teammates, who made these stories so memorable. Finally, I hope as my daughter, Madison, and my son, Dylan, get older that maybe one day they'll read this book and be proud of what their dad accomplished in life.

—Phil Bourque

To my mom—thank you for taking me to my first hockey game.

To Brad, Kayla, Colton, and Connor—thank you for being the world's four greatest children.

To Jayme—thank you for being my best friend, my person, my love.

—Josh Yohe

APPENDIX

Pittsburgh Penguins Championships

Stanley Cups	5 (1990–91, 1991–92, 2008–09, 2015–16, 2016–17)
Conference championships	6 (1990–91, 1991–92, 2007–08, 2008–09, 2015–16, 2016–17)
Presidents' Trophy	1 (1992–93)
Division championships	8 (1990–91, 1992–93, 1993–94, 1995–96, 1997–98, 2007–08, 2012–13, 2013–14)

Pittsburgh Penguins Retired Numbers

No.	Player	Position	Career	No. retirement
21	Michel Briere	C	1969–70	January 5, 2001
66	Mario Lemieux	C	1984–97	
			2000–06	November 19, 1997

Pittsburgh Peguins Hockey Hall of Fame Inductees

Hall of Fame Players

Andy Bathgate
Mario Lemieux
Leo Boivin
Joe Mullen
Paul Coffey
Larry Murphy
Ron Francis
Mark Recchi
Tim Horton
Luc Robitaille

Red Kelly
Bryan Trottier

Hall of Fame Builders

Scotty Bowman
Herb Brooks
Bob Johnson
Craig Patrick

Team Captains

Ab McDonald, 1967–68
Earl Ingarfield, 1968–69
Ron Schock, 1973–77
Jean Pronovost, 1977–78
Orest Kindrachuk, 1978–81
Randy Carlyle, 1981–84
Mike Bullard, 1984–86
Terry Ruskowski, 1986–87
Dan Frawley, 1987
Mario Lemieux, 1987–94
Ron Francis, 1995
Mario Lemieux, 1995–97
Ron Francis, 1997–98
Jaromir Jagr, 1998–2001
Mario Lemieux, 2001–06
Sidney Crosby, 2007–present

Pittsburgh Penguins Career Leaders

Games Played

1.	Sidney Crosby	943
2.	Mario Lemieux	915
3.	Evgeni Malkin	852
4.	Jaromir Jagr	806
5.	Jean Pronovost	753
6.	Kris Letang	747
7.	Rick Kehoe	722
8.	Brooks Orpik	703
9.	Marc-Andre Fleury	691
10.	Ron Stackhouse	621

Goals

1.	Mario Lemieux	690
2.	Sidney Crosby	446
3.	Jaromir Jagr	439
4.	Evgeni Malkin	391
5.	Jean Pronovost	316
6.	Rick Kehoe	312
7.	Kevin Stevens	260
8.	Mike Bullard	185
9.	Chris Kunitz	169
10.	Martin Straka	165

Assists

1.	Mario Lemieux	1,033
2.	Sidney Crosby	770
3.	Jaromir Jagr	640
4.	Evgeni Malkin	611

5.	Ron Francis	449
6.	Kris Letang	381
7.	Syl Apps	349
8.	Paul Coffey	332
9.	Rick Kehoe	324
10.	Kevin Stevens	295

Points

1.	Mario Lemieux	1,723
2.	Sidney Crosby	1,216
3.	Jaromir Jagr	1,079
4.	Evgeni Malkin	1,002
5.	Rick Kehoe	636
6.	Ron Francis	613
7.	Jean Pronovost	603
8.	Kevin Stevens	555
9.	Syl Apps	500
10.	Kris Letang	493

Goals Created

1.	Mario Lemieux	649.7
2.	Sidney Crosby	444.8
3.	Jaromir Jagr	404.7
4.	Evgeni Malkin	373.0
5.	Rick Kehoe	261.3
6.	Jean Pronovost	252.9
7.	Kevin Stevens	218.0
8.	Ron Francis	207.5
9.	Syl Apps	179.3
10.	Kris Letang	162.4

Plus/Minus

1. Jaromir Jagr   207
2. Sidney Crosby   183
3. Chris Kunitz   126
4. Mario Lemieux   114
5. Larry Murphy   102
6. Syl Apps   90
7. Pascal Dupuis   82
8. Lowell MacDonald   77
9. Ulf Samuelsson   76
10. Ron Francis   70

Penalties in Minutes

1. Kevin Stevens   1,048
2. Troy Loney   982
3. Rod Buskas   959
4. Evgeni Malkin   902
5. Bryan Watson   871
6. Paul Baxter   851
7. Mario Lemieux   834
8. Gary Rissling   830
9. Ulf Samuelsson   804
10. Brooks Orpik   734

Even Strength Goals

1. Mario Lemieux   405
2. Jaromir Jagr   320
3. Sidney Crosby   307
4. Evgeni Malkin   245
5. Jean Pronovost   233
6. Rick Kehoe   216

7.	Kevin Stevens	150
8.	Martin Straka	126
9.	Mike Bullard	123
10.	Bob Errey	119

Power Play Goals

1.	Mario Lemieux	236
2.	Evgeni Malkin	142
3.	Sidney Crosby	136
4.	Jaromir Jagr	110
	Kevin Stevens	110
6.	Rick Kehoe	95
7.	Jean Pronovost	69
8.	Rob Brown	68
9.	Mark Recchi*	61
10.	Paul Gardner	59

Short-Handed Goals

1.	Mario Lemieux	49
2.	Jean Pronovost	14
	Ron Schock	14
4.	Jordan Staal	13
5.	George Ferguson	12
	Maxime Talbot	12
7.	Ryan Malone	11
	Syl Apps	11
9.	Jaromir Jagr	9
	Martin Straka	9
	Bob Errey	9

Game-Winning Goals

1.	Jaromir Jagr	78
2.	Mario Lemieux	74
3.	Evgeni Malkin	68
4.	Sidney Crosby	60
5.	Jean Pronovost	42
6.	Chris Kunitz	28
7.	Kevin Stevens	27
8.	Rick Kehoe	26
	Martin Straka	26
10.	Phil Kessel	25

Shots

1.	Mario Lemieux	3,633
2.	Sidney Crosby	3,063
3.	Jaromir Jagr	2,911
4.	Evgeni Malkin	2,874
5.	Jean Pronovost	2,311
6.	Rick Kehoe	2,160
7.	Kris Letang	1,934
8.	Kevin Stevens	1,631
9.	Ron Stackhouse	1,341
10.	Chris Kunitz	1,318

Shooting Percentage

1.	Petr Nedved	19.8
2.	Rob Brown	19.7
3.	Mike Bullard	19.1
4.	Mario Lemieux	19.0
5.	Paul Gardner	19.0
6.	Craig Simpson	18.8

7.	Joe Mullen	17.8
8.	Mark Recchi	17.4
9.	Jan Hrdina	17.0
10.	Rick Tocchet	16.9

Hat Tricks

1.	Mario Lemieux	40
2.	Evgeni Malkin	12
3.	Sidney Crosby	11
4.	Kevin Stevens	10
5.	Jaromir Jagr	9
6.	Alex Kovalev	8
	Rick Kehoe	8
8.	Rob Brown	7
9.	Mike Bullard	6
10.	Martin Straka	4
	Lowell MacDonald	4
	Pierre Larouche	4
	Joe Mullen*	4

Goals per Game

1.	Mario Lemieux	0.75
2.	Jaromir Jagr	0.54
3.	Rick Tocchet	0.51
4.	Petr Nedved	0.51
5.	Kevin Stevens	0.50
6.	Pierre Larouche	0.50
7.	Mike Bullard	0.48
8.	Paul Gardner	0.47
9.	Sidney Crosby	0.47
10.	Evgeni Malkin	0.46

Assists per Game

1.	Mario Lemieux	1.13
2.	Paul Coffey	1.00
3.	Ron Francis	0.84
4.	Sidney Crosby	0.82
5.	Jaromir Jagr	0.79
6.	Evgeni Malkin	0.72
7.	Syl Apps	0.71
8.	John Cullen	0.70
9.	Rick Tocchet	0.69
10.	Larry Murphy	0.66

Points per Game

1.	Mario Lemieux	1.88
2.	Jaromir Jagr	1.34
3.	Paul Coffey	1.33
4.	Sidney Crosby	1.29
5.	Rick Tocchet	1.19
6.	Evgeni Malkin	1.18
7.	Ron Francis	1.15
8.	Petr Nedved	1.10
9.	Kevin Stevens	1.06
10.	Pierre Larouche	1.05

Goals Created per Game

1.	Mario Lemieux	0.71
2.	Jaromir Jagr	0.50
3.	Sidney Crosby	0.47
4.	Rick Tocchet	0.46
5.	Paul Coffey	0.45
6.	Evgeni Malkin	0.44

7.	Petr Nedved	0.43
8.	Pierre Larouche	0.43
9.	Kevin Stevens	0.42
10.	Paul Gardner	0.40

Games Played (Goalie)

1.	Marc-Andre Fleury	691
2.	Tom Barrasso	460
3.	Denis Herron	290
4.	Ken Wregget	212
5.	Les Binkley	196
6.	Jean-Sebastien Aubin	168
7.	Matt Murray	161
8.	Michel Dion	151
9.	Greg Millen	135
10.	Roberto Romano	125

Wins

1.	Marc-Andre Fleury	375
2.	Tom Barrasso	226
3.	Ken Wregget	104
4.	Matt Murray	97
5.	Denis Herron	88
6.	Jean-Sebastien Aubin	63
7.	Les Binkley	58
8.	Greg Millen	57
9.	Roberto Romano	46
	Johan Hedberg	46

Losses

1. Marc-Andre Fleury   216
2. Tom Barrasso   153
3. Denis Herron   133
4. Les Binkley   94
5. Michel Dion   79
6. Jean-Sebastien Aubin   72
7. Ken Wregget   67
8. Roberto Romano   62
9. Johan Hedberg   57
10. Greg Millen   56

Goals Against

1. Marc-Andre Fleury   1,713
2. Tom Barrasso   1,409
3. Denis Herron   1,040
4. Ken Wregget   644
5. Michel Dion   605
6. Les Binkley   574
7. Greg Millen   501
8. Roberto Romano   465
9. Jean-Sebastien Aubin   432
10. Matt Murray   398

Saves

1. Marc-Andre Fleury   17,774
2. Tom Barrasso   12,076
3. Denis Herron   8,068
4. Ken Wregget   5,641
5. Les Binkley   5,038

6.	Matt Murray	4,424
7.	Michel Dion	3,999
8.	Jean-Sebastien Aubin	3,937
9.	Greg Millen	3,486
10.	Roberto Romano	3,406

Save Percentage

1.	Matt Murray	.918
2.	Marc-Andre Fleury	.912
3.	Jean-Sebastien Aubin	.901
4.	Johan Hedberg	.901
5.	Al Smith	.899
6.	Jim Rutherford	.899
7.	Les Binkley	.898
8.	Ken Wregget	.898
9.	Gary Inness	.896
10.	Tom Barrasso	.896

Shutouts

1.	Marc-Andre Fleury	44
2.	Tom Barrasso	22
3.	Les Binkley	11
4.	Matt Murray	10
5.	Johan Hedberg	7
6.	Jean-Sebastien Aubin	6
	Denis Herron	6
	Ken Wregget	6
9.	Dunc Wilson	5
10.	Sebastien Caron	4
	Al Smith	4

Peter Skudra	4
Jim Rutherford	4
Casey DeSmith	4
Roberto Romano	4
Greg Millen	4

ABOUT THE AUTHORS

Phil Bourque played for the Pittsburgh Penguins from 1983 to 1992, winning the Stanley Cup twice in that time. He currently serves as the color commentator alongside Mike Lange for Penguins radio broadcasts.

Josh Yohe covers the Penguins for The Athletic Pittsburgh. He previously wrote about the team for the *Pittsburgh Tribune-Review* and then for DKPittsburghSports.com.